HEINEMANN ADVANCED RELIGIOUS STUDIES

PHILOSOPHY *of* RELIGION

Second Edition

H J RICHARDS

Dedicated to
the sixth-formers
of Notre Dame School, Norwich,
who in the course of many years
accompanied me
as we helped each other explore
this strange and fascinating country.

Heinemann Educational Publishers,
Halley Court, Jordan Hill, Oxford OX2 8EJ
a division of Reed Educational & Professional Publishing Ltd

OXFORD   MELBOURNE   AUCKLAND
JOHANNESBURG   BLANTYRE   GABORONE
IBADAN   PORTSMOUTH (NH) USA   CHICAGO

Heinemann is a registered trademark of Reed Educational &
Professional Publishing Ltd

First published 2000

04 03 02 01 00
9 8 7 6 5 4 3 2 1

British Library Cataloguing in Publication Data
A catalogue record for this book is available from the
British Library

ISBN 0 435 30259 0

Typeset by Techset Ltd
Printed and bound in Great Britain by The Bath Press, Bath

Acknowledgements
The publishers would like to thank the following for
permission to reproduce copyright material:

OCR Examinations for the OCR examination questions used
throughout this book; UCLES for the examination questions
used throughout this book; AQA for the AQA and NEAB
examination questions used in this book; Ruqaiyyah Waris
Maqsood for the English translations from the Qur'an;
National Council of Churches of Christ in the USA for
quotations from the Revised Standard Version of the Bible
used throughout this book (all Bible quotations are from
the RSV except those acknowledged to other sources in the
text); Triangle/SPCK for the extract from 'The Gap:
Christians and People who don't go to church' by Jack
Burton (1991) on p. 10; Cambridge University Press for
extracts from the Common Book of Prayer, the rights in
which are vested in the Crown, reproduced by permission
of the Crown's Patentee, Cambridge University Press, on
pp. 11 and 12; and for the extract from the Authorized
Version of the Bible (The King James Bible), the rights in
which are vested in the Crown, reproduced by permission
of the Crown's Patentee, Cambridge University Press, on
p. 11; The Confession from An Order for Holy Communion,
Alternative Services 3, is copyright © The Central Board of
Finance of the Church of England 1971, 1973 and is
reproduced by permission on p. 12; Darton, Longman and
Todd for extracts taken from the New Jerusalem Bible,
published and copyright 1985 by Darton, Longman and
Todd Ltd and Doubleday & Co Inc, and used by permission
of the publishers on pp. 15, 17, 23, 32 and 99; Lord
Jakobovits for the quote on p. 40; *The Independent* for
extracts from 'Last Eternal Moments' by Frank Kuppner
(5/10/94) on pp. 56–7. 'Why God can allow an earthquake'
by Bishop Richard Harries (1988) on p. 58 and 'Science and
God: The Archbishop's Reply' by Archbishop T. Hapgood
(4/5/1992) on p. 67; Extracts by J.F.X. Harriott, on p. 41 and
p. 67, from 'The Tablet' 1983 and 1984. Reprinted with
permission of The Tablet: *The Times* for 'No Humankind
without disasters' by Clifford Langley, from *The Times*,
26/8/1985 on pp. 57–8(c) Times Newspapers Limited; Poem
by Alfred Noyes on p. 59. Reprinted by permission of The
Society of Authors, as the Literary Representative of the
Estate of Alfred Noyes; Extract from 'Faith, The Unutterable
Beauty' on p. 60 by G.A. Studdert Kennedy from 'Liturgy of
Life' by D. Hilton, 1991. Reprinted by permission of National
Christian Education Council; Extract from 'Peter Abelard'
on p. 60 by Helen Waddell, published by Constable 1933.
Reprinted with permission of Constable & Robinson
Publishing Limited; Extract by Philip Mason, on p. 67, from
'The Tablet' 1991. Reprinted with permission of the Tablet;
Extract by Libby Purvess, on p. 81, from 'The Tablet' 1999.
Reprinted with permission of The Tablet.

The publishers would like to thank the following for
permission to use photographs:

pp. 3, 19, J. Allen Cash; pp. 9, 64, 69, 104, Mary Evans
Picture Library; p. 15, FLPA – Images of Nature/M. Nimmo;
p. 30, Robert Harding Picture Library/Simon Harris; p. 36,
Bridgeman Art Library/National Gallery; p. 44, Bettmann/
Corbis; p. 53, Mike Wyndham; p. 58, Andes Press Agency/
Fugifotos; p. 83, Science Photo Library/US National Archive;
p. 88, Camera Press/Symil Kumar Dutt; p. 97, Bettmann/
Corbis; p. 99, FLPA – Images of Nature/JC Allen.

The publishers would also like to thank Getty Images for
permission to reproduce the cover photograph.

The publishers have made every effort to contact copyright
holders. However, if any material has been incorrectly
acknowledged, the publishers would be pleased to correct
this at the earliest opportunity

Tel: 01865 888058 www.heinemann.co.uk

Contents

Foreword

The dedication on page ii uses the metaphor of travel and exploration. Having had the good fortune to visit Jerusalem and Rome many times in order to act as leader for groups on pilgrimage, I have been able to use the experience gathered over the years to write a guidebook on each of these two places. But I have spent most of my adult lifetime in the classroom, latterly with sixth-formers, and it occurred to me that there was room here too for a guidebook written from experience.

Philosophy of Religion has in recent years become an increasingly popular option for A level students. Ideally they should be well equipped for the courses on offer, since there is no shortage of literature on the subject, both general and specialized. Unfortunately, much of this literature is aimed at a professional readership and, until recently, scant provision has been made for beginners, who can find the strange terrain not a little bewildering, and the technical language of philosophers not a little discouraging. I hope that these beginners may find what follows a little more user-friendly.

But they must be warned that what I am here offering is only an introduction, with all the shortcomings of introductions. They must read more than this short book if they intend to sit the AS and A level exams. There are suggestions for further reading, from among the books that I have myself found most helpful, on page 110.

Since the publication of the first edition of this book in 1998, radical changes have been made in the requirements for the General Certificate of Education (GCE). The multiple examination boards in England have been replaced by three new boards: the Assessment and Qualifications Alliance (AQA), the Oxford, Cambridge and RSA Examinations (OCR), and the Edexcel Foundation. Their first examinations for the Advanced Subsidiary Certificate (AS) will take place in 2001, and for the Advanced Certificate (A) in 2002. I have closely studied the syllabuses published by all three boards to ensure that their requirements are met, and appended at the end of each chapter some of the sample questions that have so far been issued. And since all three boards will give credit for appropriate examples taken from any world religion, I have incorporated many more references to religions other than Christianity than I did in my first edition.

The controversial French philosopher Denis Diderot (1713–1784) told a teasing parable:

> I am wandering through a vast forest at night, with only a candle to guide me. A stranger appears and tells me to blow out my candle in order to find my way more clearly. I ask him who he is, and he tells me. A philosopher.

Was this just a facetious comment on his own profession? Or was it a shrewd assessment of the need for all philosophers to rid themselves of their prejudices in order to find their way? After all, a candle will only illuminate the next tree, and actually blind you to the rest. Blowing it out may help you slowly to see the whole forest.

To change Diderot's metaphor, students have a right to be given an *à la carte* menu which tells them honestly what is on offer, and not forced to accept the *table d'hôte* which only tells them what the host prefers.

H. J. Richards

1 God-talk

A CONVERSATION

Sceptic

'Religious believers use a lot of puzzling words, like God, grace, heaven, soul, salvation and so on. What sort of reality corresponds to these words?

I mean, are these things real, or just in your mind? Do they exist **objectively** – independently of you?

Some people have believed in things that are only **subjective** – things that don't actually exist, like tooth-fairies and leprechauns and dragons. Would you put the Loch Ness Monster into this subjective category? Or UFOs? Or ghosts? Or devils? Or angels?

Where exactly would you draw the line between the real and the unreal, the objective and the subjective? And what reasons can you give for putting God on one side of the line instead of the other?'

> **Objective** Existing in the real world of objects, independently of you.
> **Subjective** Existing only in you (the subject), not in reality.

```
Unreal
 ↑ Tooth-fairies
   Father Christmas
   Imps
   Pixies
   Elves
   Leprechauns
   Gnomes
   Goblins
   Unicorns          Where is the
   Dragons           dividing line?
   Monsters
   Giants
   Ogres
   Witches
   Vampires
   Ghosts
   UFOs
   Aliens
   Devils
   Angels
 ↓ God
Real
```

Believer

'Perhaps objective and subjective are not the best words to use when one is discussing religion.

Being objective means looking at an object neutrally, from the outside, as an uncommitted observer. Now that is obviously a very good attitude to take towards something like maths, or physics. But it is ruinous for religion. You simply can't understand very much about religion from the outside.

To understand religion, you literally have to understand it, that is, to stand under it, to feel it, to experience it. It's like a stained glass window: it's no good trying to appreciate it from the outside. You've got to go inside the building to see what it is, let alone appreciate it.

So I'm afraid you'll never understand what I'm saying from where you're standing. You've got to commit yourself and join me where I am. Then you will see how real what I'm talking about actually is.'

Sceptic

'This is like saying I'll never be able to believe in pink elephants until I believe in them. Count me out! If you want me to commit myself to pink elephants (or to God), I need some *evidence* that we're talking about something real, and not a fantasy of your mind. Before I can say, "I believe God exists", I need some *proof* (or at least some indication) that he really does exist. If you can't provide such proof, why should anyone take you seriously?'

Believer

'Well, perhaps proof and evidence are also the wrong words to use in this context.

I can provide you with tangible proof that a parcel weighs 750 grammes, or that the human body has 206 bones, or that the Great Fire of London took place in 1666. But God simply isn't the kind of reality that can be counted, or weighed or measured.

Cameras or videotapes, or slide rules, or cassette recorders are very useful for dealing with physical things. But you wouldn't find them much use for realities like love, or relationship, or forgiveness ("Can I have six yards of forgiveness please"!) And they are absolutely no use at all for the reality of God, because by definition he **transcends** all dimensions.

> **Transcendent** That which crosses the border (*trans*) and so is beyond all description or definition.

So the kind of language that deals with proof and evidence is really rather useless for talking about God. The language of poetry, symbols and stories might serve better, since it doesn't pretend to define accurately, only to suggest, to evoke, to approximate.'

He who knows does not speak.
He who speaks does not know.
Lao Tzu, 6th century BCE

Even when we say we don't know God, we still don't know God.

Hindu saying

My thoughts are not your thoughts, and my ways are not your ways, says the Lord.
The heavens are as high beyond the earth as my ways are beyond your ways, and my thoughts beyond your thoughts.

Isaiah 55:8, about 550 BCE

Seeing God means seeing that he can't be seen. Knowing God means knowing that he can't be known. He is always totally beyond what we can know.

St Gregory of Nyssa, 331–95 CE

We speak about God, not because we know anything about him, but because the alternative is to say nothing.

St Augustine, 354–430 CE

The only thing we can understand about God is that he can't be understood. If you can grasp it, it is not God.

St John of Damascus, 675–759 CE

Let us seek to fathom those things that are fathomable, and reserve those things that are unfathomable for reverence in quietude.

Johann Goethe, 1749–1832

If I could understand religion the way I understand $2 + 2 = 4$, *I wouldn't bother with it.*

Baron Friedrich von Hügel, 1852–1925

Whereof one cannot speak, thereof one must be silent.

Ludwig Wittgenstein, 1889–1951

A beetle in a cardboard box just gets a glimpse of the fingers that feed him his daily lettuce leaf. His humanology [understanding of humans] *is more profound than our* theology [understanding of God].

Peter de Rosa, 1970

God is in your heart yet you search for him in the wilderness.

Sikh Scriptures

His daily lettuce leaf

In the beginning was God.
Today is God,
Tomorrow will be God.
Who can make an image of God?
He has no body.
He is as a word which comes out of your
  mouth.
That word! It is no more,
It is past, and still it lives!
So is God.

  A hymn of the Pygmy peoples

For discussion

Many of these quotations (not to mention the main text) refer to God as 'he'. Does this not contradict the believer's insistence that God is inexpressible?

When Moses (in Exodus 3:14) asks the name of the mysterious being talking to him out of the burning bush, he is told, 'I am who I am', in other words, 'I'm not telling'. Everything else can be named. God cannot.

Using analogy to describe God

In spite of the inadequacy of human language, the Dominican monk Thomas Aquinas (1225–74) maintained that it is possible to speak in a meaningful way about God by **analogy**.

Aquinas said that no human words about God are simply **equivocal**, that is, sounding the same but meaning something utterly different (say a bat that has wings, and a bat you hit a ball with). But neither are they ever simply **univocal**, that is, meaning exactly the same in both cases, like 'Bert is a human being' and 'Clare is a human being'. All words about God are *analogical*, that is, approximate, meaning partly the same, yet still different.

Aquinas offers an example. To say God is 'wise' is not a play on words, as if God's wisdom is something utterly different from human wisdom (equivocal). But neither is God's wisdom just like human wisdom (univocal). God's wisdom is analogical to human wisdom, similar to it but still infinitely different.

The English philosopher Ian Ramsey (1915–72) speaks in a similar way of the need to use many 'models' about God (father, judge, shepherd, etc.) as long as each is modified by a 'qualifier' (supreme, ultimate, infinite, etc.)

The result of this, of course, is that whatever we say about God – however true it may be – will always be less true than the opposite. For example, while it may be true that God is a person, it is more true to say that God is *not* a person like you and me.

Some traditions take the above saying of St Augustine to its logical conclusion, and worship God in utter silence.

A Zen story tells of the teacher who claimed he had a book which told you all you could possibly know about God. A student pleads for a loan of the book and excitedly takes it home. He opens the book to find it completely blank. Angrily he takes it back to complain, 'This book tells you nothing!' The teacher replies, 'Yes, but what a lot that tells you.'

Another Zen teacher specifies the two things required in the search for God: to realize that all efforts to find God are useless; and to act as if you didn't know that.

Apophatic theology

There is a type of theology known as **apophatic** (un-saying) theology because it insists that God is not in fact any of the things he is called.

Even theology that is more traditional prefers to use negative words beginning with *in* or *im* (not) rather than positive words about God: He is *in*visible, *in*finite, *in*comprehensible, *in*effable, *im*mortal, *im*material, *im*mutable, *im*mense, *im*passible, etc. This is known as the **via negativa**.

Hindu theology similarly keeps repeating the phrase *neti neti* (not that, not that) to make the same point.

The inadequacy of language and symbols

Muslim philosophers developed the 'double negative' (God is not a being, but he is also not a non-being) in order to emphasize the inadequacy of language to express the mystery of God.

The Jewish, Muslim and Puritan traditions forbid the use of images (pictures, statues, etc.) because these could give the impression that divine realities can be represented and defined. The Hindu tradition is generally happy to keep images, confident that everyone realizes how inadequate these are, and asking theologians whether they think their abstract words are more adequate!

In short, God being what he is, the infinitely inexpressible, we can only talk about him indirectly and at a remove. Our words and ideas are only stand-ins for a reality which is always beyond us. Our symbols, signs, metaphors and images are not to be thought of as anything more than symbols, signs, metaphors and images. They only point to God, put us in touch with God, lead to God. They should never be confused with the unfathomable reality of God himself. If someone is pointing to something in the distance, he will not thank you for continuing to look at his finger. Those who are impressed by the description of a meal in a menu, and then eat the menu, will usually be disappointed.

Sceptic

'Oh come on, be serious! I'm trying to have a reasoned philosophical discussion and all you can talk about is stories and poetry!

Cut the poetry, I'm looking for the *truth*. All I'm asking is whether your statements about God are true or not.'

Believer

'And again I have to ask whether truth is the best word in this context.

I don't ask of a piece of poetry whether it is true or false. It either speaks to me or it doesn't. A truth is only something that you can *know*, and in knowing it you have made it somehow smaller than yourself. You have grasped it. But when you are stretching out to something greater than yourself, you do something more than know it. You *love* it. It grasps you.

God is not something you know. He is someone you love. Believers don't say, "I believe *that*" and trot out a string of truths. They say, "I believe *in*", meaning, "I commit myself to". The God they commit themselves to simply would not be God if he wasn't at the same time loved.'

The Christian Creed (The 'Apostles' creed')
I believe in *God the Father Almighty ...*
And in *Jesus Christ his only Son our Lord ...*
I believe in *the Holy Spirit ...*
                    Book of Common Prayer

Sceptic

'All right, you've come clean. God is nothing more than what you happen to believe in!

And since there are no means of testing whether what you believe in is real, presumably anything goes!

Tom believes in a high-fibre diet, Tracey believes in the Abominable Snowman, and Harry believes in God. None of these can be called better or worse than any of the others because there is no way of checking. Any nonsense can claim to be a 'religious belief' because there is no appeal.

If you want *your* belief in God to be taken seriously, you must surely be able to give some reasons, some evidence that it is worthwhile. I know human language may be inappropriate, but surely some language must be less inappropriate than others. Please give me some!'

Believer

'I can't unless, as I said earlier, you join me in my experience of God.

Have you never had an experience so profound that you couldn't describe it to anyone who hadn't shared it, or who wasn't at least sympathetic to you? I assure you that if you'd had the same experience of God that I have had, you'd agree that we're not talking about something unreal, but *more* real than anything else in our experience, however difficult it may be to prove to an outsider.

It is only figures with three dimensions that can understand what talk of a third dimension means. A two-dimensional figure can't. It might ask whether it is a question of extra length or breadth, not realizing however many squares you put next to each other, you will never make a cube. And the temptation might be to say, "Cubes don't exist; there is no known dimension for them to exist in." And, of course, if you can only measure in length and breadth, there isn't. The trouble with religious sceptics is that they are flat-earthers!'

Kierkegaard also said that truth is 'subjective'. By this he did not mean that it doesn't matter what we think or believe. He meant that the really important truths are personal. Only these truths are 'true for me'.

Could you give an example of a subjective truth?

An important question is, for example, whether Christianity is true. This is not a question one can relate to theoretically or academically. For a person who 'understands himself in life,' it is a question of life and death. It is not something you sit and discuss for discussion's sake. It is something to be approached with the greatest passion and sincerity.

Understandable.

If you fall into the water, you have no theoretical interest in whether or not you will drown. It is neither 'interesting' nor 'uninteresting' whether there are alligators in the water. It is a question of life or death.

I get it, thank you very much.

So we must therefore distinguish between the philosophical question of whether God exists, and the individual's relationship to the same question, a situation in which each and every man is utterly alone. Fundamental questions such as these can only be approached through faith. Things we can know through reason, or knowledge, are according to Kierkegaard totally unimportant.

I think you'd better explain that.

Eight plus four is twelve. We can be absolutely certain of this. That's an example of the sort of 'reasoned truth' that every philosopher since Descartes had talked about. But do we include it in our daily prayers? Is it something we lie pondering over when we are dying? Not at all. Truths like those can be both 'objective' and 'general', but they are nevertheless totally immaterial to each man's existence.

What about faith?

You can never know whether a person forgives you when you wrong them. Therefore it is existentially important to you. It is a question you are intensely concerned with. Neither can you know whether a person loves you. It's something you just have to believe or hope. But these

> *things are more important to you than the fact that the sum of the angles in a triangle is 180 degrees. You don't think about the law of cause and effect or about modes of perception when you are in the middle of your first kiss.*
>
> J. Gaarder, *Sophie's World*

In short, it is quite irrational to make an absolute of rationality. Reality is not confined to what is subject to reason. There are such things as values, norms, imperatives, ultimates – and these are also part of reality.

Feuerbach is famous for his assertion that God is only a projection, that is to say, a fantasy built up by those dissatisfied with real life. But while it is true that God can only be experienced as a projection, it does not follow that there is no reality behind such experience.

For discussion
Have you any beliefs for which you can't give a convincing reason?

Sceptic

'Pass! So, let me put my point the way a Logical Positivist might do.

Everyone agrees that there are only two kinds of meaningful statements: those you verify by defining (e.g. 'two plus two equals four') and those you verify by experiment or testing (e.g. 'this tea has gone cold'). Into which category do you want to put religious statements? If it's the first, then you're simply saying the same thing twice. If it's the second, then you must offer some proof. If you refuse, then I have to conclude that your religious statement is simply devoid of meaning.'

Believer

'What do you mean, "Everyone agrees that there are only two kinds of meaningful statements"? That may have been what some philosophers were saying in the 1940s, but today almost everyone who has given any thought to the matter agrees that it's a ridiculous oversimplification.

To begin with, there's absolutely no way of verifying the statement that no statement is meaningful unless it can be verified!

But more importantly, it is now agreed that there can be any number of different meaningful statements, just as there can be any number of different games. But you have to play each game by its own rules, not by the rules of another game. Tennis can only be played by tennis rules. Play it by the rules of tiddlywinks and it becomes nonsense. To find the meaning of a language, you have to ask those who use it.

The Positivist rules to language are valid only for statements which can be verified. But verification doesn't say anything about meaningfulness.'

Logical Positivism
In the 1840s the French philosopher Auguste Comte held that all true knowledge must be based on what is *positive*, that is, on what can be observed, scientifically tested and shown to be factual. Anything outside of that is sheer speculation, and not to be relied upon.

In the 1940s this principle was applied to logic and language by A. J. Ayer, A. Flew, A. McIntyre and others. Calling themselves Logical Positivists (or Linguistic Philosophers), they held that no statement can be called meaningful unless it can be similarly tested and shown to be true (verified).

Analytic statements are those that can be verified or falsified simply by analysing the meaning of the words.
'Twelve divided by three equals four.'
'This bachelor is a married man.'
'The word "God" includes "good".
Therefore God is good.'

Synthetic statements are those than can only be verified or falsified by observation and examination.

'Fred measures 5 feet 11½ inches.'
'When you ignite TNT it explodes.'
'This man has six wives.'
'Heavy smoking improves your health.'

If religious statements fall into neither category, then they are neither true nor false, but simply meaningless and literally non-sense.

A parable puts this Positivist viewpoint persuasively. Two explorers come across a clearing in the jungle. Because there are some flowers, one of them concludes that a gardener has been at work. Since there are many weeds, the other disagrees. So they set watch. In fact, no gardener ever appears. 'Perhaps he is invisible.' They fence off the plot with barbed wire, but it never moves. They electrify the wire but no shocks are registered. They patrol the plot with bloodhounds, but the dogs never bark. 'Well, perhaps he is not only invisible, but also intangible, immune to shocks, soundless and scentless.' But with that number of qualifications, how different is such a gardener from no gardener at all? Logical Positivists claimed that God has also died this 'death of a thousand qualifications'.

In the 1960s this powerful attack on religion began to diminish, particularly under the influence of the teaching and writings of the Cambridge philosopher Ludwig Wittgenstein (1889–1951).

Himself once one of the pioneers of Logical Positivism, Wittgenstein later came to see that there are *dozens* of ways in which language is used by people, not only two. He also realized that the question of 'verification' simply does not arise when people are issuing a command, or telling a joke, or asking a question, or thanking, or cursing, or greeting, or praying, or saying, 'I ought to visit my sick mum'.

To say of a given sentence that it can be verified doesn't say anything about it being meaningful, only that it is a sentence *of one particular type*, namely verifiable, testable, empirical. But there are many other types of language, and to find out their meaning, you must ask the people who use them.

Only believers can tell you what they mean by the religious language they use. So ask them. And when they talk to you about the eye of God, don't start asking questions about eyebrows.

It is interesting that in 1976, 40 years after A. J. Ayer had published his *Language, Truth and Logic* in which he claimed that Logical Positivism had demolished philosophy for ever, he was asked about any faults he now acknowledged in the book. He replied, 'Well I suppose the most important defect is that nearly all of it was false.'

For discussion

If you felt a certain sympathy for Logical Positivism, would Wittgenstein's criticism change your mind?

THE LANGUAGE OF MYTH AND WORSHIP ▪▪▪

WHAT kind of language is most appropriate for talking about God? The question is deeply felt when it comes to a discussion of myth and worship.

Myth

Reference was made on page 2 to the fact that religious language is more appropriately expressed in poetry and stories than in abstract statements. This is because the totality of life cannot be captured by simple facts and statistics. The truth about life cannot be mapped out in definitions. To state something with dead accuracy is to know it like that, dead.

The living truth cannot be grasped with the intellect alone, it also needs to be known by the emotions and feelings, by intuition and experience, in the bones and the belly, not only in the brain. And living truth of this sort is better served by a true-to-life story than by precise definitions. A page of statistics may be far more accurate than a picture of a starving child. But there is no question which conveys the truth more faithfully. The definition of the divinity of Christ made by all Christian bishops gathered in the Council of Chalcedon in 451 CE is far more precise than the Gospel stories of his resurrection, but it is to these stories that believers will turn to express their faith and reflect on it.

Not that it is a question of either one or the other. We will always need both fact and symbol, both precision and story. Without disciplined definitions, our life would be reduced to chaos. But without the inspiration of stories, our life would lack an essential dimension. And this is particularly true of the eternal drama in which all of us are engaged, where the stories we tell are called **myth**.

The word 'myth' has had a bad press. Because what myths say is not to be taken literally they have, for many people, become synonymous with lies, falsehoods, delusions. 'It is a myth that' means that the story should be dismissed as rubbish.

But myths were never proposed as 'tall stories'. They are better described as deep stories. They were never meant to be taken literally, like newspaper reports. On the other hand, they were (and continue to be) meant to be taken most seriously, because they deal with realities so profound that no scientific language can express them.

Myths are the superhuman stories through which humans interpret the world and understand their place in it. Myths speak of what people believe is most true and meaningful, what they think is eternal and original, what they hope will happen, and what they see as ultimately real, however terrible that reality may be. The characters in myths are larger than life because they are archetypes. The 'once upon a time' of

myths is not a dateable occasion in the past or the future, but the timelessness in which things are *always* so, and ultimately true.

In this sense, myths deal with insights far deeper than could be provided by history or logic or science. There is nothing more real than the myths people live by; just as the dreams people have may indicate more truly what they most hope for, and most fear, than anything they might say or do in their more rational waking hours.

To take a concrete example. When the Christian belief in a Last Day of Judgement is called a myth, it does not mean that such a day will never come. On the contrary it means that, even if such an actual day never dawns, it stands as a most potent symbol of a divine judgement taking place at every moment. The relationship between good and evil is not something trivial. It is of *ultimate* importance. Christians believe that God's victory over evil is *eternally* true. There is no way of proving or verifying this. But those who live by such a story have an entirely different attitude to life from those who don't.

Myths, then, are 'true' not in the sense that what they speak of actually happened, or will happen, but in the sense that they express truly what is *always* happening. The stories of Perseus rescuing Andromeda, or of Orpheus journeying to the underworld, or of Oedipus tragically murdering his father, or of Prometheus eternally punished for cheating the gods, or of Mithras slaying the bull to make the earth fertile – these were never told (or understood) as simple pieces of history. The stories go far deeper than that. (See also other creation myths on pages 77 and 79.)

So, of course, do the stories of Jesus coming into our history *as if* from another world, engaging in cosmic combat with a Satan who comes *as if* from an underworld, shedding his blood *as if* this were a ransom demand to liberate the human race, ascending *as if* back to that other world, where he bides his time before he will return *as if* in glory. Such stories are heavy

Mithras slaying the bull

with meaning. But that meaning can be lost if the stories are treated as simple news items.

Scholars speak of the need to 'de-mythologize' religious language. It is not a happy word, since it suggests that religious stories must be stripped of their mythical elements before what they are really saying can emerge. But this cannot be done. Myths must be accepted whole and they must be accepted *as* myths, that is to say, as profound stories which deal with people's deepest concerns. Living as we do in a world where only what can be weighed and measured tends to be taken seriously, we need to be told again and again that myth is *not* that sort of reality. It is something far more important and powerful.

> *Art is the telling of truth, and is the only available method of the telling of certain truths.*
>
> Iris Murdoch, *The Black Prince*
>
> *Art is a lie which makes us realise the truth.*
>
> Picasso
>
> *Man is never literal in the expression of his ideas except in matters most trivial.*
>
> Rabindranath Tagore
> (Indian philosopher and poet)

> *The thing about a myth is not whether it is true or not, nor whether it should be true, but that it is somehow truer than truth itself.*
>
> Thomas Kenneally, *Schindler's Ark*

For discussion
What stories do you know which are deeply true, even though they are not 'true stories'?

Worship

The problem of 'God-talk', of how to speak intelligibly of a reality which is by definition totally beyond us, is acute at the best of times. It becomes most acute when we turn from theology to worship, from talking *about* God to talking *to* him, or imagine him talking to us.

For believers, no human language can do justice to God. All of it, even the best, is quite inadequate. Presumably some of it is less inadequate than others. But what language can we possibly put into the mouth of God to express the fact that he reveals himself and his will to us? And what is the appropriate language for humans to use to make their response?

The problem is particularly pressing in the present century, when the Bible ('Word of God') has undergone dozens of translations and retranslations out of fear that the older versions have gone dead on people; and these efforts have been matched by countless reforms of the language and forms of prayer used in Christian worship.

What criteria ought to be used in such reforms? In translating the Bible or the Qur'an, for example, is accuracy and intelligibility more important than beauty? What should have priority, a down-to-earth simplicity, or a sense of awe and otherworldly transcendence? In worship should words like 'thee' and 'thou', 'vouchsafest', 'absolveth', 'eschew', 'vain doctrine', etc., continue to be used because they give an irreplaceable sense of continuity with the past? Or should they be discontinued because they no longer make sense to people of today? What is lost when rituals of venerable antiquity are 'updated'? And is what is lost compensated for by what is gained? For some believers, archaic language is essential because ordinary and everyday language destroys the sense of God. So, until recently, Roman Catholic services continued to be held in Latin. Muslims continue to refuse any other language than the original Arabic for readings from the Qur'an, claiming that no human translation can capture its divine overtones. Yet for others, antiquated language simply switches them off.

It is extremely difficult to hold the correct tension between the divine and the human, the sacred and the secular, the past and the present. Both must be catered for in the worship of a God who communicates with humans and asks for a human response. Always starting with the sacred might mean never reaching the secular, and only keeping the mystery by mystifying. On the other hand always starting with the secular might mean remaining at the level of the superficial and never reaching the sacred. The question which must always be asked is, 'What sort of language lifts the heart and brings God close, and what keeps God remote and irrelevant?' Perhaps different people will always give different answers to such questions.

It goes without saying (and this is the warning given by prophets throughout history, Jesus included) that it is quite possible to say the holiest words and do the holiest activities, and still be utterly at odds with God.

I use a new translation of the Bible when I believe it will help to make God more real and less remote. That is the test... In worship the second-rate has no place. It has crept in – and the third- and fourth-rate with it!... Worship is not ruined by heresy. It is ruined by absence of any sense of occasion.

J. Burton, *The Gap*

What is the use of words?
Consider these
(We've heard them many, many times)
That 'God' so 'loved' the world
That he 'gave' his 'only-begotten Son'
That whoso 'believeth in him'
Shall have 'everlasting life'.
These words hold truth.
These words are quite inadequate.
These words are almost inaccessible.
But these are all we have.

W. S. Beattie as quoted in
D. Hilton, *Word in Season*

In what sort of language ought people to speak to God?

The Lord's Prayer (Matthew 6: 9–13)

Our Father which art in heaven,
hallowed be thy name,

thy will be done,

in earth as it is in heaven.
Give us this day our daily bread,

and forgive us our trespasses,
as we forgive them that trespass against us,

and lead us not into temptation,
but deliver us from evil.
For thine is the kingdom,
the power and the glory,
for ever and ever.

Book of Common Prayer, 1549

Father in heaven,
may we honour here on earth
every sign of your presence,
every act of your rule,
every item of your plan,
as it stands in heaven.
Give us what we need each day,
a day at a time,
and forgive us our offences,
in the same measure as we forgive those
who have wronged us.
Do not bring us to a testing
which is beyond our power to withstand.
For you have the power and the authority;
and the glory
is for ever yours.

Contemporary Prayers, 1967

Psalm 42 (41)

As the hart panteth
*   after the waterbrooks,*
so panteth my soul
*   after thee, my God ...*
my tears have been my meat ...
Deep calleth unto deep
at the noise of thy waterspouts.

Authorized Version, 1611

Like the deer that yearns
*   for running streams,*
so my soul is yearning
*   for you, my God ...*
my tears have become my bread ...
Deep is calling on deep
in the roar of waters.

Grail Version, 1963

Confession

Almighty God,	*Almighty God,*
Father of our Lord Jesus Christ,	*our heavenly Father,*
Judge of all men,	
we acknowledge and bewail	
our manifold sins and wickedness	*we have sinned against you*
which we most grievously have committed	
by thought, word and deed,	*in thought and word and deed*
provoking most justly	*through ignorance, weakness*
thy wrath and indignation.	*and our own deliberate fault.*
We do earnestly repent,	*We are truly sorry and*
and are heartily sorry	*repent of all our sins . . .*
for these our misdoings;	
the remembrance of them	
is grievous unto us;	
the burden of them	
is intolerable . . .	
Forgive us all that is past.	*Forgive us all that is past.*
Book of Common Prayer, 1549	*Alternative Services, Series 3, 1973*

For discussion

Compare some of the quotations set alongside each other in the boxes above. In each case, which version speaks to you more than the other?

SAMPLE EXAM QUESTIONS

1 'Analogy is inadequate in conveying the greatness of God.' Discuss.

(OCR AS sample paper)

2 'In assessing the meaningfulness of religious statements, the verification principle is useless.' discuss.

(OCR AS and A sample paper)

3 Discuss critically the strengths and weaknesses of myth in expressing human understandings of God.

(OCR A sample paper)

4 Discuss critically the use of symbol as a means of expressing ideas about God.

(OCR A sample paper)

5 'Religious language can be understood only in the context of religious belief.' Discuss and evaluate this claim with reference to language games.

(Edexcel A sample paper)

6 'If we claim to understand God, then what we understand is not God.' Discuss.

(UCLES 1993)

Does God exist?

Is it possible to prove that God exists? Chapter 1 expressed considerable hesitation about this. But not everyone has shared that hesitation. Throughout history arguments have been put forward claiming to demonstrate conclusively that God exists, or at least claiming to lead the honest enquirer towards that conclusion.

A PRIORI AND A POSTERIORI ARGUMENTS

IN presenting these arguments the distinction is sometimes made between *a priori* and *a posteriori*, and between inductive and deductive arguments.

An *a priori* argument is one which is based on a general principle, before (*prior*) any evidence is produced. If someone steps off the pavement into the path of a bus doing 50 mph, I don't need any evidence to know that he or she will be hurt. In contrast, an *a posteriori* argument is made only after (*post*) something has actually been experienced. The argument goes from effect to cause. When I get a sharp pain in my chest, I can argue that something has gone wrong, like indigestion, or a heart attack, or a bullet wound.

An *inductive* argument works from a number of instances to infer a general rule, presuming that future instances will resemble past ones. A waiter who has always got a tip after serving his customers will expect one from the next customer. The argument is reasonable enough, but is obviously weaker than a *deductive* one, which follows necessarily and without exception from what precedes, as a logical consequence. If all Manx cats are by definition tailless, then I can safely deduce that the Manx cat I have just won in a raffle will have no tail.

In what follows, the Ontological Argument is *a priori* and inductive. Whether the other arguments are strictly *a posteriori* and deductive needs to be discussed.

THE ONTOLOGICAL ARGUMENT

THIS argument is based on the very being (*ontos*) of God, and works *a priori* or from the top down. It is most famously associated with St Anselm, Archbishop of Canterbury, 1093–1109.

Anselm maintained that it is possible to argue for the existence of God from the very meaning of the word 'God'. He claimed that one cannot think of God as *not* existing. He claimed that existence is essential to the very idea of God. Here are his own words.

We believe that God is a being than which none greater can be thought. Now even a fool knows that 'a being than which none greater can be thought' exists at least in his mind. But clearly, 'that than which a greater cannot be thought' cannot exist in the mind alone. It could be thought of as existing in reality as well, and that would be greater. In which case, 'that than which a greater cannot be thought' would be that than which a greater can be thought! Since this is impossible, there obviously exists, both in the mind and in reality, something than which a greater cannot be thought.

Proslogion, chapter 2, 1078

In short, the word 'God' refers to *the* perfect being. But if this did not exist, it would not be perfect. Therefore it must exist.

Or, in shorter still, God is too good not to be real.

This ontological argument has fascinated philosophers down the ages, and new forms of it continue to appear even today.

René Descartes (1596–1650) added his own observation that, just as a triangle would not be a triangle unless its angles added up to 180°, so God would not be God if he did not exist. Gottfried Leibniz (1646–1716) and Georg Hegel (1770–1831) both defended the ontological argument. Paul Tillich (1886–1965) spoke of God as 'Ultimate Reality', about whose nature people could disagree, but not about whether it exists.

More recently, Norman Malcolm (1911–1990) held that if the concept of 'God' implies a Being whose existence is necessary, then either a Being with this property cannot fail to exist, or the concept is meaningless. Alvin Plantinga (b. 1932) argues that since it is possible for an utterly Perfect Being (he uses the term 'a being of maximal excellence') to exist in every possible world, and our world *is* a possible world, it is not irrational to claim that such a Being exists.

How convincing is the ontological argument?

The argument has always had its critics. In Anselm's own day, a fellow monk, Gaunilo, accused him of making an illegitimate jump from existence in the mind to existence in reality. On such an argument, he said, one could define anything into existence, including a perfect holiday island! In short, it is cheating to hide the idea of existence in the word 'God', so that when you unwrap it you find that he exists.

David Hume (1711–76) dismissed the *a priori* argument as even more worthless than *a posteriori* arguments, which he considered quite inconclusive.

The German philosopher Immanuel Kant (1724–1804) insisted strongly that the word 'exists' may not be used as a simple predicate (quality) of God. The word 'God' may indeed include 'goodness', 'almightiness', 'wisdom', etc. but not 'existence'. That needs to be proved.

'Pixies *are* little men with pointed hats' does not mean that pixies *exist*! Or as Kant himself put it, '$100 in my mind does not mean they exist in my wallet'. We need *reasons* for believing in the existence of God, and not simply a definition of what God might be *if he existed*.

THE COSMOLOGICAL ARGUMENT

*T*HIS argument is based on the kind of world (*cosmos*) we live in, and works *a posteriori* or from the bottom up. Its popularity can be gauged from its antiquity and universality. All cultures, at all times, have proposed that, by simply looking at the world, we can argue to the existence of its creator.

The Hebrew Book of Psalms contains the lovely lines:

The sky proclaims God's glory,
its dome his handicraft:
day to following day,
night to following night,
tells his story.
No speech, no words,
no human voice is heard,
yet their music echoes across the world,
their speech to remotest peoples.

> Psalm 19: 1–4, translated by
> A. T. Dale, *Winding Quest*

The Greek philosopher Aristotle (384–322 BCE) argued that if there is movement and change, then there must be an 'Unmoved Mover' a remote and unchanging Being who allows his world to be changeable so that it can gradually move towards the perfection which he already enjoys.

The sky proclaims God's glory

The Book of Wisdom, written in Egypt about 50 BCE, says:

Naturally stupid are all who are
  unaware of God,
and who, from good things seen,
have not been able to discover
  Him-who-is …
If they are capable of acquiring
  enough knowledge
to be able to investigate the world,
how have they been so slow to find its Master?

Wisdom 13: 1–9, *New Jerusalem Bible*

The Jew Saul of Tarsus, who became a Christian as St Paul, wrote to his fellow Christians in Rome in 58 CE:

God has made himself known
  to all everywhere
through the world which he has made;
this is plain for all to see …
Nobody can say,
'We can't possibly know anything about God.'
As we can learn what a man is like
from the things he has made,
so we can learn what God is like
from what God has made.

Romans 1: 18–20, translated by
A. T. Dale, *New World*

The Qur'an, which Muslims believe is God's word as revealed to Muhammad in the 7th century CE, uses a similar argument.

In the creation of the heavens and the earth and the alternation of night and day, and the ship that runs in the sea with profit to men, and the water God sends down from heaven … and the turning about of the winds, and the clouds compelled between heaven and earth – surely there are signs for a people having understanding.

Qur'an 2: 158ff

The quotation expresses a respect for human reasoning which was developed by the Muslim scholastics of the 10th century CE, especially by Al-Ashari (878–941 CE), founder of the school of theology known as **Kalam**. The school was strongly dependent on the works of Aristotle, which had been translated into Arabic at a time when they remained almost totally unknown to Western theologians. *Kalam* means 'discourse' or 'argument', and was used to suggest that God is known not only because he has revealed himself, but also because the God-given human powers are able to argue to his existence (though not to his nature). *Kalam* therefore took a middle course between the conservative traditionalists for whom God's utter transcendence renders him knowable by faith alone, never by reason, and this *Mutazilite* school which claimed that reason is the only criterion of truth.

For discussion

Is it possible to find out anything worthwhile about a person from an examination of one of their hairs? Can God really be known from inspecting the natural world?

The person most commonly associated with the cosmological argument in the West is Thomas Aquinas (1224–74), himself dependent on Aristotle through these Arab philosophers. He takes as his starting point three facts of common experience in our cosmos: change, causality and dependence. He then proceeds to argue as follows.

In the cosmos as we experience it, it is obvious to us that some things change (or are caused, or are dependent). Now, whatever changes (or is caused, or is dependent) must be changed by (caused by, dependent on) another. And if that other itself changes (is caused, is dependent), then that too must be changed by (caused by, dependent on) another. But this cannot go on to infinity, because then there would be no change (causality, dependence) going on at all. You eventually have to arrive at something that is Unchanging (Uncaused, Non-Dependent).
This is God.

Summa Theologiae I, 1, 3

The word that Aquinas uses for change is 'movement'. He sees changing things as moving from one state into another.

The word he uses for dependency is 'contingency'. A contingent being is one that happens to exist but needs not do so ('here today, gone tomorrow'), unlike God who is the 'Necessary Being'.

The advantage of the cosmological argument is that it is based on the ordinary experiences with which anyone can identify. Why is this ball moving? And what made the racquet hit it? And what brought the tennis player into existence? And so on. Anyone demanding a *total* explanation of anything whatever, and pursuing the question further and further back, has to arrive at an ultimate answer. This is called the 'Principle of Sufficient Reason'.

This questioning cannot go on for ever ('Infinite Regress') because there can be no explanation of any present activity unless the ultimate cause is at work *here and now*. The buck cannot be passed on and on – it has to stop somewhere. The movement of railway carriage Z may be explained by carriage Y pulling it, and the movement of Y by carriage X pulling it, etc. But none of the carriages would be moving at all unless somewhere there is an engine not pulled by anything else.

How convincing is the cosmological argument?

Aquinas never pretended the argument had any kind of knock-down force. He never called his three arguments 'proofs', but 'ways' – roads which lead to some conclusion, invitations to explore the implications of the world we live in. Like Anselm, he was addressing himself to believers, not to unbelievers.

The trouble is that it is not believers who need this argument, only unbelievers. And since these are not looking for any explanation of the cosmos, the whole argument seems rather pointless. For those who don't believe in God, the cosmos is simply 'a brute fact', as the Cambridge philosopher Bertrand Russell (1872–1970) called it. Things simply are as they are.

In any case, if the whole force of the argument is that everything requires an explanation, then one can logically ask, 'What is the explanation of God? Who caused him?' And to reply, 'He is outside the series of explanations' sounds like a cop-out.

In short, people must make up their own minds about which is the more likely or the more satisfying: a world which is its own explanation, or a world which needs something outside of it to explain it.

THE TELEOLOGICAL ARGUMENT

THE Greek world *telos* means distance (telephone means speaking from a distance; television means seeing at a distance). The teleological argument is based on the observation that the things we see in our world not only come from somewhere, but seem to be going somewhere. Our world is not just haphazard, chaotic, chance. Things seem to have a *distant* purpose, an aim, an end.

There is an orderliness about the universe – the recurring seasons, the design of a seashell, the intricacy of an eyeball, the complexity of the human brain, etc. – which argues for a divine Designer or Architect (i.e. God).

Like the cosmological argument, this argument from design has been put forward in many forms throughout history.

In the Bible, the first chapter of the book of Genesis (written about 550 BCE) describes the whole world as the result of an orderly and carefully prepared creation taking place over two lots of three days. In the first three days the world is distinguished into separate compartments: light–darkness, sky–sea, and dry land. In the second three days these compartments are furnished with the heavenly lights, with the birds and sea beasts, and the animals and humans. The repeated phrase says it all: 'God saw that it was good', that is, orderly, harmonious, well-proportioned.

The book of Job (from about 500 BCE) presents the argument as a series of questions.

Where were you when I (God) laid the
*   earth's foundations? . . .*
Who decided its dimensions, do you know?
Or who stretched the measuring line across it?
What supports its pillars at their bases?
Who laid its cornerstone
to the joyful concert of the morning stars? . . .
Who pent up the sea behind closed doors . . .
when I cut out the place decreed for it? . . .
Which is the way to the home of the Light,
and where does darkness live?

>   Job 38: 4–19 *New Jerusalem Bible*

One of the biblical psalms of roughly the same date puts it this way.

You (God) fixed the earth on its
*   foundations,*
for ever and ever it shall not be shaken . . .
From your high halls you water the
*   mountains,*
satisfying the earth with the fruit of your
*   works:*
for cattle you make the grass grow,
and for people the plants they need,
to bring forth food from the earth,
and wine to cheer people's hearts . . .
You made the moon to mark the seasons,

the sun knows when to set.
You bring darkness and night falls.

>   Psalm 104: 5–20, *New Jerusalem Bible*

Aristotle in particular (4th century BCE) was a strong supporter of the argument from design. We are in the dark about the purpose of many things in life. But there are many more that are so clearly purposeful that one can only conclude that behind the changing universe stands an Ultimate Designer – static, impassive and eternal.

The classical form of this argument was put by Thomas Aquinas (1224–74).

(This argument) is taken from the
orderliness of the world. We see that all
things, even those that lack knowledge, act
for a purpose. This is evident from the fact
that they act always (or nearly always) in
the same way, in order to obtain the same
result. So it is clear that they achieve their
purpose by design, not by chance. Now
things that lack knowledge cannot move
purposefully unless they are directed by
some intelligent being: an arrow needs an
archer to shoot it. Therefore there must
exist some intelligent being who directs all
things to the purpose for which they exist.
This being we call God.

>   *Summa Theologiae* I, 1, 3

F. Copleston (b. 1907) paraphrases:

We observe material things of very different
types cooperating in such a way as to
produce and maintain a relatively stable
world order . . . But non-intelligent material
things certainly do not cooperate
consciously in view of a purpose . . . Their
cooperation clearly points to the existence
of an extrinsic intelligent author of their
cooperation, who operates for a purpose. If
Aquinas had lived (today), he would
doubtless have argued that the evolutionary
hypothesis supports rather than invalidates
the conclusion of the argument.

>   *Aquinas*, Penguin, 1961, p.125

Two quaint observations come from later times.

Nature has made the hindermost parts of our body which we sit upon most fleshly, as providing for our ease, and making us a natural cushion.

H. More, *An Antidote Against Atheism*, 1659

The ribs on melons were designed by a wise God so that they can be divided up among a family at table.

Bernadin de St Pierre, 1715

Some hymns which use the same argument

The earth with its store of wonders untold,
Almighty, thy power hath founded of old;
hath stablished it fast by a changeless decree
and round it hath cast, like a mantle, the sea.

Thy bountiful care what tongue can recite?
It breathes in the air, it shines in the light;
it streams from the hills, it descends to the plain,
and sweetly distils in the dew and the rain.

R. Grant (1779–1833),
Hymns Ancient and Modern, 167

All things bright and beautiful,
all creatures great and small,
all things wise and wonderful,
the Lord God made them all.

The cold wind in the winter,
the pleasant summer sun,
the ripe fruits in the garden,
he made them every one.

He gave us eyes to see them,
and lips that we may tell
how great is God Almighty,
who has made all things well.

C. F. Alexander (1818–95)
Hymns Ancient and Modern, 442

For the beauty of the earth
for the beauty of the skies,
for the love which from our birth
over and around us lies,
Lord of all, to thee we raise
this our grateful hymn of praise.

F. S. Pierpoint (1835–1917)
Hymns Ancient and Modern, 171

When the ozone layer around the earth was first discovered, many believers acclaimed it as a further piece of evidence of a teleological world. This layer of gas absorbs most of the sun's harmful ultra-violet radiation and so makes life on earth possible. Who but a wise Designer could have arranged this?

Most recently the **Anthropic Principle** has been greeted in a similar way. This principle states that the Genesis picture, of a universe deliberately designed for human beings, is confirmed by science. A universe hospitable to humans is dependent on so many hairline conditions (the slightest deviation in any of them would have wrecked the end result) that it cannot be put down to sheer chance.

Paley's watch

The most famous form of the teleological argument was proposed in 1802 by the Archdeacon of Carlisle, William Paley. Here are his words.

In crossing a heath, suppose I pitched my foot against a stone, and were asked how this stone came to be there, I might possibly answer that, for anything I knew to the contrary, it had lain there for ever ...

But suppose I found a watch ... I should hardly give the same answer ... Why should not this answer serve for the watch as well as for the stone? For this reason: when we come to inspect the watch we perceive (what we could not discover in the stone) that its several parts are framed and put together for a purpose, e.g. that they are so formed and adjusted as to produce motion, and that motion so regulated as to point out the hour of the day; that, if the different parts had been differently shaped from what they are, or placed after any other manner ... either no motion at all would have been carried on in the machine, or none which would have answered the use that is now served by it. ... This mechanism being observed ... the inference, we think, is inevitable, that the

To point out the hour of the day...

> *watch must have had a maker... who formed it for the purpose which we find it actually to answer; who comprehended its construction, and designed its use.*
>
> *Nor would it weaken the conclusion that we had never seen a watch made... or that the watch sometimes went wrong, or that it seldom went exactly right... or if there were a few parts of the watch concerning which we could not discover... in what manner they conducted to the general effect...*
>
> *Every manifestation of design, which existed in the watch, exists in the works of nature... only greater and more and exceeding all computation... The contrivances of nature surpass the contrivances of art, in the complexity, subtlety, and curiosity of the mechanism.*
>
> *Natural Theology,* chapter 3

For discussion

Does Paley's argument impress you? Are there any details that you would criticize?

How convincing is the teleological argument?

The argument has enjoyed a great vogue throughout history, and continues to be appealed to more readily than any other argument. Even Immanuel Kant (1724–1804) reckoned it was the oldest, clearest and most reasonable of all the arguments for the existence of God, though he himself found it unconvincing. But there is a danger of turning the argument from design on its head. Human arms were not divinely designed to be at the exact level of door-handles – it was the other way round. Hen's eggs are not providentially planned to fit exactly into egg-cups – it is the other way round.

The rise of modern science has raised even more question marks. The world revealed to us by Darwin's studies in evolution is not as benign and providential as we may have naïvely imagined. It continues to be 'red in tooth and claw', the provisional product of irrepressible chance forces across millions of painful years, and still evolving into new and unknown forms. Darwin himself wrote:

> *This immense and wonderful universe cannot be the result of blind chance... I feel compelled to look to a First Cause... But then arises the doubt: Can the mind of man, which has, as I fully believe, been developed from a mind as low as that possessed by the lowest animals, be trusted when it draws such grand conclusions?*
>
> From a letter to a friend

More recently, scientific research into what is known as **Chaos Theory** is beginning to undermine Newton's optimistic view of the universe as a predictable machine (see page 70). It is not in fact (we now discover) made up of building blocks obeying 'laws of nature', but of waves and impulses whose activity is anyone's guess, even when they continue to provide a coherent whole.

If a pattern does eventually emerge, could it be simply nature's way of surviving? Those who fit into the pattern survive, the rest perish. Who is to say that the human race is not the survivor of a million failed worlds? If God stands behind such a world, he is something far more mysterious than a clever watchmaker.

The biologist Richard Dawkins (b. 1941) writes:

In a universe of blind physical forces and genetic replication, some people are going to get hurt, other people are going to get lucky, and you won't find any rhyme or reason in it, nor any justice. The universe we observe has precisely the properties we should expect if there is, at bottom, no design, no purpose, no evil and no good, nothing but blind pitiless indifference.

R. Dawkins, *River Out of Eden*

Moreover, if some of the universe seems well designed, there is much that is sheer bad design: reckless wastage, painful childbirth, death by mischance, universal death in any case, etc. What Grand Designer would invent a race of dinosaurs to dominate planet Earth for 140 million years, and then simply obliterate them? If natural disasters are added (flood, drought, earthquake, volcanic eruption, plague, disease, infant mortality, etc.) one could question the wisdom and goodness of the Designer. J. S. Mill (1808–73) waxed eloquent on this subject (see page 51).

Even if it could be proved that there *is* design in our world, who can tell (as the Scottish philosopher David Hume (1711–76) asked) whether the Designer is not plural, or stupid, or downright evil? Or whether the order we see is imposed on the chaos in which we live by humans insistent on finding a pattern and a meaning?

In the light of such considerations, more recent forms of the teleological argument (such as those proposed by F. R. Tennant (1866–1957) and Richard Swinburne (b. 1934)) are less absolute than those of the past. An intelligently designed universe cannot be *proved*, but it is more *probable* than a universe ruled by blind forces or chance. How can the sheer orderliness, uniformity and predictability of our world be put down to mere coincidence? A purposeful Designer cannot be proved to exist, but is a more plausible and satisfactory explanation of the evidence we have than any other.

> **For discussion**
> Do you find that this toning down of the Teleological Argument makes it weaker or stronger?

THE MORAL ARGUMENT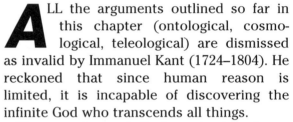

ALL the arguments outlined so far in this chapter (ontological, cosmological, teleological) are dismissed as invalid by Immanuel Kant (1724–1804). He reckoned that since human reason is limited, it is incapable of discovering the infinite God who transcends all things.

However, he said, God *can* be found in a practical way through our experience of 'ought', 'should' and 'must':

> I *ought* to go and help; he'll never manage on his own.
> I *should* stop nagging her: she's doing her best.
> I *must* do my homework before I watch any more telly.

Since this sense of obligation is universal, and since we didn't invent it (or even want it), we have to speak of an absolute and unconditional claim that makes us act only on what we would wish to be a universal law. Kant calls this the **'Categorical Imperative'**.

Because this claim over-rides any other claim we experience, its source (concluded Kant) must be transcendent. This is God, the Moral Governor of the Universe. Conscience is his voice, telling us what is right and wrong.

How convincing is the moral argument?

Different cultures differ considerably about what is right and wrong, good and evil. Cannibals clearly don't hear the same 'voice' as vegetarians, or polygamists the same as monogamists, or Jephthah the same as Jesus (see the Book of Judges, chapter 11). This suggests (as Freud analysed) that the 'voice' is far more dependent on education, self-interest, desires and needs than Kant allowed.

There may come times when we have to disregard what the 'Categorical Imperative' is commanding (for example, 'Thou shalt not kill') in order to do something even more urgent – as when the theologian Dietrich Bonhoeffer collaborated in a plot to kill Hitler in 1945. Can the 'voice of God' contradict the 'voice of God'?

Finally, one must ask what it is that makes atheists and agnostics act responsibly and morally, even without a Moral Governor?

PASCAL'S WAGER

THE French philosopher Blaise Pascal (1623–62), realizing that none of the classical arguments provided a knock-down proof for the existence of God, opted for an alternative way of approaching the question.

He argued that, although reason cannot prove God exists, reason tells us that it would be wiser to act as if he *does* exist, rather than as if he doesn't. If it turns out that he does exist, than I shall have lived a good life and enjoy a blessed eternity. I shall have gained everything. And if he doesn't exist and there is no eternity, then I shall never know. I shall have lost nothing.

In short, God's existence is a more worthwhile bet than his non-existence.

Let us say: 'Either God is, or he is not.' To which view shall we be inclined? Reason cannot decide this question. Infinite chaos separates us. At the far end of this infinite distance, a coin is being spun which will come down heads or tails. How will you wager? Reason cannot make you choose either. Reason cannot prove either wrong . . .

But you must wager. There is no choice . . . Let us weigh up the gain and the loss involved in betting that God exists. Let us assess the two cases: if you win you win

everything, if you lose you lose nothing; wager then that he does exist . . .

Wherever there is infinity, and where there are not infinite chances of losing against that of winning, there is no room for hesitation, you must give everything. And thus, since you are obliged to play, you must be renouncing reason if you hoard your life rather than risk it for an infinite gain, which is just as likely to occur as a loss amounting to nothing.

Pascal, *Pensées*

How convincing is Pascal's argument?

Not many philosophers have been impressed by Pascal's reasoning. Some have strongly objected that there is something squalid about believing in God in order to come out on the winning side, and even something blasphemous about coming to a belief in God on the toss of a coin.

Perhaps a good test of the argument would be to ask people whether they would bet on Pascal's wager or not, and why. Few would feel able to live with a God who is the object of a bet; fewer still would feel able to worship him on this basis.

A further argument for the existence of God, often used, is based on the actual experience of God that people claim to have had. This is more complex than the arguments so far considered, and will be dealt with in chapter 4 (see p. 35).

SAMPLE EXAM QUESTIONS

1 Explain Kant's version of the moral argument for the existence of God. How far have psychological explanations of religious beliefs disproved such moral arguments?

(OCR AS sample paper)

2 To what extent is it important for religious believers to challenge 'scientific' views of the world?

(AQA AS sample paper)

3 Explain Paley's argument for the existence of God.

(AQA AS sample paper)

4 What are the strengths and weaknesses of the teleological arguments for the existence of God? To what extent can modern scientific theories be said to have disproved the claim that the universe has been designed?

(OCR AS sample paper)

5 How far do modern versions of the ontological argument succeed in overcoming the weaknesses of Anselm's version?

(OCR A sample paper)

6 'The ontological argument is an *a priori* proof and, as such, cannot inform us about the world.' Explain and assess this claim.

(OCR A sample paper)

What sort of God?

The *nature* of God is logically prior to the *existence* of God. Before I can answer the question, "Does God exist?" I have to know what sort of reality I am talking about. What sort of qualities should God possess to be God-like?

GOD IS ONE

> **Pantheism** The belief that God is everything (*pan*) and everything is God.
>
> **Polytheism** Belief in many (*poly*) gods, each responsible for a different department of life.
>
> **Henotheism** Belief in many gods, of whom only one (*henos*) is chosen to be worshipped (*monolatry*).
>
> **Monotheism** Belief in a single (*monos*) God, excluding all other claimants to the title.

The ancient Egyptians, Mesopotamians, Greeks and Romans were polytheists; they worshipped many gods, as do a vast number of people in the Far East today. Such believers emphasize the plurality and diversity of the life they live. In contrast, Christians and Muslims have inherited from Judaism an emphasis on the unity of things, and believe in one and only one God.

> *Hear, O Israel:*
> *The Lord our God is one Lord;*
> *and you shall love the Lord your God*
> *with all your heart and all your soul,*
> *and with all your might.*
>
> Deuteronomy, 6: 4–5

This belief was the end product of a long development in Israel. The earliest texts in the Bible speak of Israel's God 'Yahweh' as a tribal God, in competition with the gods of other nations. This *henotheism* did not become a full-blooded *monotheism* until about 500 BCE. Witness a piece of writing from that time:

> *He who sits enthroned above the circle of*
> *the earth,*
> *on which the inhabitants are like*
> *grasshoppers,*
> *stretches out the heavens like a cloth . . .*
> *and reduces princes to nothing . . .*
> *Yahweh is the everlasting God,*
> *he creates the remotest parts of the earth . . .*
> *I, Yahweh, am the first,*
> *and till the last I shall still be there . . .*
> *No god was formed before me*
> *nor will be after me.*
> *I, I am Yahweh*
> *and there is no other Saviour but me . . .*
> *I am the first and I am the last;*
> *there is no God except me.*
>
> Isaiah 40: 22–44: 6, *New Jerusalem Bible*

Or this, from the Qur'an:

> *There is no God but He, the Living, the Self-subsisting, the Eternal.*
>
> Surah 2: 225

There are important consequences to such a development. If God is no longer the God of one group but the single universal God, then:

- he excludes all rivals: if there is a Devil, he cannot be absolute, like God
- he has absolute priority over all other loyalties

- he makes the same ethical demands of everyone
- he abolishes the distinction between sacred and secular: there are no 'no-go' areas.

GOD IS PERSONAL

Note – It is important to use the adjective 'personal' rather than the noun 'person'. To believers, God is not a 'person', to be numbered alongside other persons. God is not even a 'superperson', a human being magnified to the *n*th degree. God simply cannot be spoken of as a thing or object.

But, to believers, he *is* personal. That is to say, he is not *im*personal, or *sub*personal, or *less* than personal. He is not an 'it' (a Pool of Energy, a Force, a Power, etc.) but a 'thou', who can relate to people as people can to him, and who is felt and experienced as close and intimate.

He is therefore more accurately represented in personal terms than the impersonal ones used by philosophers – Ground of Being, Unmoved Mover, First Cause, Necessary Being, etc. In the Bible, God is never impersonal, always personal, as the quotations in the following box demonstrate.

> *Arise O Lord, deliver me O my God*
>
> Psalm 3:7
>
> *Be gracious to me, O Lord*
>
> Psalm 6:2
>
> *When I look at thy heavens,*
> *what is man that thou art mindful of him?*
>
> Psalm 8:3
>
> *Why dost thou hide thyself, Lord?*
>
> Psalm 10:1
>
> *I heard the voice of the Lord saying,*
> *'Whom shall I send and who will go for us?'*
> *Then I said, 'Here am I! Send me.'*
> *And he said, 'Go, and say to this people'*
>
> Isaiah 6:8

> *The Lord put forth his hand and touched*
> *my mouth,*
> *and the Lord said to me,*
> *'Behold, I have put my words in your mouth.'*
>
> Jeremiah 1:9
>
> *The word of the Lord came to the prophet*
> *Zechariah,*
> *'Thus says the Lord of hosts:*
> *Return to me and I will return to you.'*
>
> Zechariah 1:3
>
> *O God, no one grants pardon for sins except*
> *you.*
> *Forgive me therefore in your compassion,*
> *for you are the Forgiver, the Merciful.*
>
> Muslim private prayer

So strong is this conviction that God is personal that the Jewish Bible does not hesitate to speak of him in thoroughly human terms (**anthropomorphism**). God is a lover, a husband, a father, a mother, a shepherd, a king, a judge, etc. God walks with Adam in the garden, shuts the door of the Ark behind Noah, holds back the Red Sea for Israel, etc. God is even pictured as angry, jealous, frustrated, ignorant of the future, able to change his mind...

Such anthropomorphisms have always embarrassed philosophers. Surely such language is far too primitive and childish to do justice to God? Surely the abstract language of philosophy is more appropriate?

But philosophers forget that *all* language about God is inappropriate and inadequate, including their own. Anthropomorphism that is openly recognized as *only* anthropomorphism at least speaks of a God who is near, not remote, who is involved with his world, not indifferent to it. Anthropomorphism can be seen as a first inkling of what Christians speak of as **incarnation**.

These anthropomorphisms, of course, are not easily reconciled with the next attribute to be considered – God's holiness.

GOD IS HOLY ━━━━━

THE word in the Hebrew Bible which we have translated as 'holy' is in fact far stronger than the word 'holy' is in our language. It has nothing to do with being pious, devout or virtuous. Less still with being narrow, austere or church-going. In Hebrew, holy means 'different', other, separate, sacred.

The holy is *so* different from anything we have otherwise experienced that it is hair-raising, awesome, dangerous – the philosopher Rudolf Otto called it the mystery which terrifies (*mysterium tremendum*). What it first inspires in us is not admiration but fear. We can usually cope with things that are different and unfamiliar in the long run. The holy *never*. It will always be other, totally beyond us, the numinous, the unknown.

The point is strongly made in the Hebrew Torah stories of Moses meeting God in the desert, and of Isaiah's vision of God in the Temple (see page 36). The Christian New Testament makes the same point in the story of Simon Peter:

> *Jesus said to Simon, 'Put out into the deep, and let down your nets for a catch.' And Simon answered, 'Master, we toiled all night and took nothing! But at your word I will let down the nets.' And when they had done this, they enclosed a great shoal of fish... and they filled both the boats, so that they began to sink. But when Simon Peter saw it he fell down at Jesus' knees, saying 'Depart from me, for I am a sinful man. O Lord.'*
>
> Luke 5: 4–8

In spite of this, the *mysterium tremendum* is also *fascinans*, that is, attractive, alluring. Holiness is like fire: it repels and attracts at the same time.

All believers in a holy God have given expression to this holiness by designating certain places, persons, days, seasons and objects as separate, different, 'holy'. In fact,

the whole nation of Israel, committed to such a holy God, felt itself under obligation to be holy (Leviticus 11: 45) that is, separate, different. Of course this separateness does not easily harmonize (for Israel) with love of one's neighbour, or (for God) with omnipresence.

Other words to express God's holiness:
transcendent going beyond everything
infinite without any limits
perfect without any defects
and compounds of *omni* ('all') such as

    omnipresent
    omnipotent
    omniscient

and compounds of *im* or *in* ('not') such as:

    immortal
    immutable
    immense
    immaterial
    impassible
    invisible
    incomprehensible
    ineffable.

GOD IS OMNIPRESENT ━━━

STORIES of bi-location are told of some of the saints: they were said to be present in two locations at the same time. God is said to be omni-located, present everywhere and absent nowhere, unlike the pagan gods who had no clout outside their own shrine, or at most outside their own country.

This attribute of God, like his holiness, has both awesome and comforting overtones, as the following quotations illustrate:

> *O Lord, you search me and you know me...*
> *all my ways lie open to you...*
> *Behind and before you besiege me,*
> *your hand ever laid upon me...*
> *Where can I go from your spirit,*
> *or where can I flee from your face?*
> *If I climb the heavens, you are there.*

If I lie in the grave, you are there.
If I take the wings of the dawn
and dwell at the sea's furthest end,
even there your hand would lead me,
your right hand would hold me fast...
Search me, God, and know my heart...
see that I follow not the wrong path.

Psalm 139, *Grail Version*

I am with you whenever you mention Me.
If you draw near to Me by only a
 handsbreadth,
I draw near to you by an armslength.

A saying of Muhammad

GOD IS OMNIPOTENT ▬▬

GOD is said to be *potens* (able) to do
omne (everything).
Some philosophers (e.g. Descartes,
1596–1650) would include under this
heading even contradictions ('God could
make a square circle') and illogicalities
('God could make $2 + 2 = 5$'). God is beyond
our limited human logic, and with him *all*
things are possible.

But most theologians would hold that God is
only able to do all *possible* things (not the
impossible, which is a non-being), and only
able to do all that is *consistent* with his nature.

From this it follows that the omnipotent
God *cannot* do something unloving since, by
definition, he *is* love (1 John 4: 16). His
almightiness is the omnipotence of love. He
is omnipotent and unconquerable, but only
by loving. Love does not win by compulsion,
but by attraction and evocation.

There is no violence, distress or hardship,
there is no persecution, hurt or pain,
there are no principalities or powers,
there is no threat, not even death itself,
that can unmake the love we've seen in Jesus.
Nothing can ever take away from us
the love of God that we have seen in Christ.

Romans 8: 35–9,
translated by H. J. Richards

In short, the omnipotence of God must not
be used to turn him into a despot ruling by
naked force. His 'lordship' must not turn
everyone else into slaves. And his power
must be reconcilable both with the free will
of his creatures and with the persistent
existence of evil.

The omnipotence of God establishes him as
the sole Creator of all that exists. Everything
is dependent on him, the Independent One.
And his creativity is quite unlike the human
activity of 'creating' from something that
already exists. God creates out of *nothing*.
This means that it is *into* nothing that all
would fall it if was not constantly upheld by
him. Existence itself is a grace, a gift. And
creation is a constantly ongoing progress.

Bless the Lord, my soul!
Lord God, how great you are...
You founded the earth on its base,
to stand firm from age to age...
From your dwelling you water the hills;
earth drinks its fill of your gift.
You make the grass grow for the cattle
and the plants to serve our needs...
All of these look to you
to give them their food in due season.
You give it, they gather it up:
you open your hand and they have their fill.
You hide your face, they die,
returning to the dust from which they came.
You send forth your spirit, they are created;
and you renew the face of the earth.

Psalm 104, *Grail Version*

To God belongs everything in heaven and
on Earth and he has power over all things.

Surah 2: 284

A God who is as intimately related to and
involved with his creation as this, is not far
from the Christian doctrine of incarnation,
or 'God-made-man'. And there can be
optimism about a creation that is in such
safe hands, and has such a sure direction.
The Original Goodness of all things is more
important than Original Sin (see page 53).

GOD IS OMNISCIENT

GOD is said to be *sciens* (knowing) of *omne* (all, not only in the present but in the past and future too).

> *God has the key of the unseen, the treasures none know but he. He knows whatever is on land or in the sea: no leaf falls without his knowing it.*
>
> Surah 6:59

Such a God can reveal the future to his friends – prophecy is often accepted as proof that one is a spokesperson for God. Such a God is also able to foresee, and so be provident. His world is not haphazard, the result of chance, but designed for the benefit of his creatures, whom his providence protects.

Some difficulties

- Can a spiritual God know what can only be known by bodies (heat, physical pain, etc.)?
- An already known future seems to be pre-determined and fixed. If so, what price freedom? And how could my sufferings be a test of my faithfulness if the result is already known? And why should I bother to pray about a tomorrow which is already decided?
- John Calvin (1509–64) spoke of a fixed number of souls being predestined for heaven, and the rest for hell. Jehovah's Witnesses hold a similar doctrine. The alternative would seem to be that heaven is achieved by human effort, not by God's decree. Pelagius was condemned as a heretic for saying this in the 5th century CE.

Some answers

- If everything is already determined, then so is Calvin's deterministic viewpoint. An own goal!
- A God *outside* time would not strictly *foresee*. He would simply timelessly see, in an unchanging present, the result of our free choice. To see this, as if from a mountain top, is in no way to cause it.
- Perhaps the absolute *omni*-words which we have borrowed from Greek philosophy are inappropriate for God.

GOD IS IMMORTAL

GOD would not be God if he could die (i.e. if he was mortal). Since he is self-existent, uncaused, uncreated and totally independent, God must be deathless. The phrase 'death of God' is a contradiction in terms: whatever it was that died, it could not be God.

> *God is eternal and absolute, the unborn. There is no one like him.*
>
> Surah 112
>
> *There is only one God, the Creator, timeless and without form.*
>
> Sikh Scriptures

Philosophers disagree about whether such a God should be called 'timeless' or 'eternal'.

A *timeless* God (such as the Greek philosopher Plato envisaged) would exist entirely *outside* time, which is simply one of his creations, like everything else. All God's activity would take place in a present which has no 'before' or 'after'. Such a God could not change, because change can only take place in time.

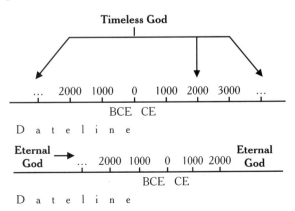

An *eternal* or everlasting God, even though existing before time began and after it finishes, could co-exist *with* and *in* time as long as it was there, and would be as limited by it as anyone else. Such a God could not know the future because, even for him, it would not yet exist (see page 27).

GOD IS GOOD ▬▬

I T was the Greek philosopher Socrates (469–399 BCE) who first pointed out that God's goodness poses a dilemma.

Who decides what is good?
If it is God, then presumably he could call
    lying good, and it would be.
Who wants a God like that?
If it is not God, since he has to obey a higher
    law just as we do, then he is not supreme.
Who wants a God like that?

The problem is a false one. In the almost universal understanding of God, goodness is not something external to him. Goodness is what he is *identified* with. Goodness is what the word 'God' *means*. He could no more cease to be good than he could cease to be God.

Hence, in the Hebrew Bible, God is celebrated in terms of **hesed** and **rahamim**. *Hesed* means loving kindness, merciful compassion, and is used prodigally throughout the psalms (26 times in Psalm 136). *Rahamim* is a most remarkable word to use of God. It refers to the gut-feeling of pity and tenderness that a mother feels for her unborn child.

For Christians too, God is identified with the Greek word **agapé** – an outgoing love, which wants only the welfare of the beloved, the opposite of **eros** which wants the beloved only for oneself. St John says it all:

God so agape *the world*
that he gave his only Son.

John 3: 16

Everyone who has agape
is like God, his Father
and knows God for what he is.
Because what God ultimately is, is agape.
Anyone who does not practise agape
Has never really experienced God.

1 John: 47–8

Who is God? Not omnipotence but... encounter with Jesus Christ. His being for others is the experience of transcendence... Our relation with God is not a 'religious' relationship to the most powerful Being imaginable – that is not authentic transcendence. It is a new life in being for others. The transcendent is not an unattainable task, but (simply) the neighbour, always within reach. God comes in human form, not as a terrifying animal... not as abstract infinity... but as the man for others, *the crucified one. That is what transcendence is about... The Church is only the Church when it (too) exists* for others... *To live with Christ means to exist for others.*

Dietrich Bonhoeffer,
Letters and Papers from Prison (1945)

In the name of God, the compassionate, the most merciful and most kind.

Opening words of the Qur'an

If it is true that this gracious and loving kindness is the nearest we can get to defining what God actually is, then the other attributes we have applied to God must be rethought. His omnipotence, for example, can no longer be thought of as the naked power of a tyrant (as already noted on page 26), but only as the almightiness of a love which nothing can ever overcome. God's power cannot be thought of as a threat to human freedom.

Similarly his omniscience can no longer be thought of as absolute. It has to be limited by his loving commitment to a time-bound creation, whose future is always open. God knows the future only because he knows that his love will always be victorious.

Nor does this idea of the 'goodness' of God contradict the 'justness' of God. According to the Jewish Bible, God does not practise a blind and impartial letter-of-the-law justice. He is just to *himself*. He will never be inconsistent with his own gracious nature. That is why God's justness (or righteousness, as the Bible calls it), far from contradicting his love or mercy, is in strict parallel with it, as the following quotations show:

Steadfast love *and faithfulness will meet,* righteousness *and peace will kiss each other.*

Psalm 85: 10

Righteousness *and justice are the foundation of thy throne,* steadfast love *and faithfulness go before thee.*

Psalm 89: 14

His righteousness *endures for ever, the Lord is gracious and* merciful.

Psalm 111: 3–4

Gracious *is the Lord and* righteous.

Psalm 116: 5

They shall pour forth the fame of thy adundant goodness, *they shall sing aloud of thy* righteousness . . . *The Lord is* just *in all his ways, and* kind *in all his doings.*

Psalm 145: 7, 17

For discussion

The difficulty remains of reconciling all that has been said under the heading 'God is good' with texts which speak of God's wrath, rage, anger, vengeance, retaliation, punishment of sinners, etc. Are such texts to be dismissed as second-class and primitive? Or are they trying to say something about the seriousness of sin, which would bring all hell about us were it not for God's love?

GOD IS IMMUTABLE ■■■■

BY definition, what is perfect cannot change (mutate) for the better, or indeed for the worse. Being perfect, God is said to be immutable.

The Hebrew word used in the Bible to express this quality of God is *eme(n)th*, which is often translated as 'truth' but means firmness, solidity, reliability, dependability. God is unchangeable in the sense that he is true to his promise, trustworthy. The Hebrew response to this fact is *amen(th)*, meaning 'That's for sure', 'You bet!'. The Book of Revelation 3: 14 calls Christ 'God's Amen' – the guarantee that he keeps his word.

The Hebrew word for this quality of God is therefore a *concrete* one. God had been experienced as reliable and constant in the actual events of history. Greek philosophy was not based on historical experience, but on the *abstract* thought which says: 'Nothing is totally reliable unless it is totally unchanging.' So God's reliability came to be thought of as unchangeability. This, of course, raised several problems:

- it is difficult to see what relation there could be between such a timeless and changeless God and a world which is essentially timebound and changing
- how relevant is a non-suffering God in a world that suffers?
- can an invulnerable God be a truly loving God?
- does not the Christian teaching about incarnation ('God becoming man') involve change?

If the Gospels present an utterly vulnerable Jesus as the truest picture of God, what does that tell us about God?

The Jewish Torah is not in the least embarrassed to speak of a loving God as being vulnerable, moved with compassion, full of tenderness and pity. For example:

Can a woman forget her sucking child,
that she should have no compassion
on the son of her womb?
Even these may forget,
yet I (God) will not forget you.

Isaiah 49:15

Is Ephraim my dear son?
Is he my darling child?
For as often as I speak against him,
I do remember him still.
Therefore my heart yearns for him,
I will surely have mercy on him,
says the Lord.

Jeremiah 31:20

How can I give you up, O Ephraim!
How can I hand you over, O Israel!...
My heart recoils within me,
my compassion grows warm and tender.

Hosea 11:8

Praise God who forgives all our sins...
he clothes us in mercy and love,
Our God is all kindness and love,
so patient and rich in compassion...
As fathers take pity on sons,
we know God will show us compassion.

Psalm 103: 3–13,
translated by H. J. Richards

This is echoed in Islamic teaching:

One man said to another:
'By God, God will never forgive him.'
At this, Almighty God said: 'Who
is this who swears by me that I
will never forgive someone? In fact,
I have forgiven him already.'

From the sayings of Muhammad

For discussion

In your view, do these descriptions of God in personal terms downgrade or upgrade God?

Some theologians have recently been asking whether the philosophical idea of perfection

The Forth Bridge

(timelessness, changelessness, remoteness) has hidden God from us, rather than revealed him. They point out that, while a perfect bridge may be changeless, a perfect artist cannot be. A perfect crossword-solver may solve her puzzle totally, but a perfect teacher must constantly adapt. A perfect engine may repeat the same movement over and over, but a perfect chess-player would always be looking for new variations.

The sort of perfection spoken of by the philosophers is *static*. It has little to do with our own experience, where all reality is change, movement, activity, process. Is it not more likely that the Ultimate Reality is *dynamic* like that?

Certainly that is what is presumed in the Bible, whose God echoes the warmth of human hearts, so that he can be angry and surprised and disappointed, and even change his mind. These anthropomorphisms (see page 24), say the theologians, are not to be dismissed as primitive naïvety: they serve to remind us that God is personal and dynamic, not a static object; a close friend and companion, not an abstract lawgiver.

Recent **Process Theology** has therefore turned its back not only on **Pantheism** (God is indistinguishable from his creation), but also on **Theism** (God is divorced from his creation). Instead, theologians such as Alfred Whitehead (1861–1947), Charles Hartshorne (b. 1941) and Schubert Ogden

(b. 1966), speak of **Pan-en-theism**, where God is so involved with his creation that he is in it, and it is in him. Such a God, being affected by everything that happens, and influenced by it, and enriched by it, is himself in process, and by no means unchangeable. Nor can he be immune to suffering – he suffers in and with his creatures. Jesus preached about a God who is affected by the death of every twopenny-halfpenny sparrow (Matthew 10: 29).

OTHER WAYS OF TALKING ABOUT GOD

One of the difficulties about much of what has been said in chapter 2 about the existence of God, and in this present chapter about the nature of God, is that again and again the 'God' we have been discussing has been 'thingified', turned into an object to be closely inspected through a telescope or dispassionately analysed under a microscope.

Unfortunately, this sort of 'God' – distant, detached, dispassionate – has little to do with what actual devotees of God believe in. It is not that the arguments were shaky. But even if the arguments were cast-iron, what they would have proved has little to do with religion.

The traditional arguments were all based on the philosophy of Plato and Aristotle (see page 96). This philosophy produced the 'Perfect Being', the 'Unmoved Mover', the 'Uncaused Cause', the 'Necessary Being', the 'Divine Designer', the 'Moral Governor', and the 'Best Bet'. But none of these is enough to bring believers to their knees. What believers are looking for is a God who can be worshipped.

In short, all the questions we have so far asked have treated God as an *object*. Whereas the truth is that God is not an object alongside other objects (e.g. 'there are 25 people in this room, plus God, that makes 26'). God is a subject met by a subject, or as the Jewish philosopher Martin Buber (1878–1965) puts it, a 'Thou', not an 'It'.

Philosophers ask whether God exists outside the religious context, out there, independently of the observer. Believers reply that their God is not the kind of reality which can be shown to exist outside the religious context.

Are there ways of talking about God which do not turn him into an object? Are there ways of talking about God which might be more appropriate (or at least, less inappropriate) than the ones we have tried so far? Here are some suggestions.

God as shining through people

How can you doubt whether God exists when the person you are talking about is patently standing in his presence? Or is the godliness shining out of some people a mere illusion?

God as embodied in everything that exists

The cosmological argument says that you can argue for God's existence *from* things that exist, as if you had to make a journey from one to the other. Would it not be more true to say that these things *are* God, showing his face in a million different ways?

> *My Beloved* is *the mountains,*
> *the solitary wooded valleys,*
> *the strange islands,*
> *the wooded torrents,*
> *the whisper of the amorous gales,*
> *the tranquil night.*
>
> St John of the Cross (1542–91)

God as a verb rather than a noun

St John's definition of God as love (see the following box) identifies him as an activity rather than a substance or object. In other words, God is wherever there is loving going on. When people say 'God is with us', they are not talking about a *person* dwelling in their midst, but about a godly *life* that they share with one another. In short, God is not something that people make their way to, but rather something that happens to them on the way.

> Love is from God,
> and everyone who loves
> is a child of God
> and knows God.
> Whoever fails to love
> does not know God,
> because God is love...
> As long as we love each other
> God remains in us...
> God is love,
> and whoever remains in love
> remains in God,
> and God in him.
>
> > 1 John, 4: 7–16 (1st century CE),
> > *New Jerusalem Bible*
>
> God may well be loved, but not thought;
> by love he may be caught,
> but by thinking never.
>
> > *Cloud of Unknowing* (14th century CE)

God as ground of being

The use of the word 'transcendent' (literally 'rising above') has tended to locate God 'out there', in another world, at an infinite distance. The American theologian Paul Tillich (1886–1965) suggested it might be better to see God as the reality people stand on, what people are rooted in, the deepest dimensions of their lives; not 'up there' but 'down here'. He called such a God the 'ground of being' in something of the way of the psalms which speak of God as the 'rock' on which the whole of reality is supported.

This would mean that the real atheists are not those who say there is no God, but those for whom *nothing* is deep, who say that love is nothing, and justice is nothing, and loyalty is nothing, and wisdom is nothing (see page 106).

God as the future

Most images of God place him in the past, as Creator, Father, Source, where things come *from*. But God can be thought of as that which people are making their way *to*. In which case, God is that which draws and lures all things beyond their present limitations, into as yet unknown possibilities.

> Blowing through heaven and earth, and in our hearts and the heart of every living thing, is a gigantic breath – a great Cry – which we call God. Plant life wished to continue its motionless sleep next to stagnant waters, but the Cry leaped up within it and violently shook its roots: 'Away, let go of the earth, walk!'...
>
> It shouted in this way for thousands of eons; and lo! as a result of desire and struggle, life escaped the motionless tree and was liberated.
>
> Animals appeared – worms – making themselves at home in water and mud...
>
> But the terrible Cry hammered itself pitilessly into their loins. 'Leave the mud, stand up, give birth to your betters!'
>
> 'We don't want to! We can't!'
>
> 'You can't, but I can. Stand up!'
>
> And lo! after thousands of eons, man emerged, trembling on his still unsolid legs.
>
> > Nikos Kazantzakis (Greek novelist, 1885–1957), *Report to Greco*

God as the canvas

One of the shortcomings of traditional images of God is that they separate God too absolutely from his world. Would it help to envisage God as the canvas on which the whole of history is being painted? Or the world as the song of which God is the singer? Or the cosmic dance of which God is the dancer? In none of these cases is it possible to think of the universe without God, since it would have no reality apart from him. And it would be as pointless to try to prove the existence of God as it would for James Bond to prove the existence of Ian Fleming.

God as the sum of our values

Some 'non-realist' theologians today insist that God is not an object, an individual, a being existing in the way that a chair does. God is not a reality of that kind at all.

This does not mean that they think of God as *un*real. He is the name they give to what they find most real, creative and affirmative in their lives: love, compassion, justice, truth, goodness, beauty – even though these realities do not actually exist as separate 'beings'.

God as mystery

The word God, even for educated people, has become so tied up with the Church, preaching, moralizing sermons, 'God rammed down your throat', God the Thunderer, God up there, God 'made in man's image and likeness', God 'sponsoring the murder of our brothers and sisters' – that for many people the word no longer produces light, only darkness. And since all God-talk is inadequate in any case, perhaps the most fitting way to 'speak' about God might be to keep silent.

If words are thought unnecessary, they should be hesitant and tentative, with the awareness of Aquinas that whatever we say about God can only be analogical, that is, however true, always less true than the opposite (see page 3).

> *Immortal, invisible, God only wise,*
> *in light inaccessible hid from our eyes . . .*
> *all laud we would render: O help us to see*
> *'tis only the splendour of light hideth thee.*
>
> W. Chalmers Smith (1824–1908),
> *Hymns Ancient and Modern*, 372
>
> *Eternall God, for whom we ever dare*
> *seeke new expressions, doe the Circle square,*
> *and thrust into strait corners of poor wit*
> *thee, who art cornerless and infinite . . .*
> John Donne (1572–1631),
> *Fount Classic Poems*

God as known only by experience

God is not the sort of reality that can be known from a distance, like mathematics. You don't need to be involved or committed to 'know' maths. God is more like a language which you can only know through long usage and years of practice. Knowledge of God is more like knowledge of a person, whom you can never really know as a mere object, but only by becoming involved – the deeper the better (see chapter 4).

Conclusion

This section began with the suggestion that there was something unsatisfactory about the preceding pages. The danger is that there may be something unsatisfactory about this section as well! If the reality of God can be as imprecise, ambiguous and vague as is now being suggested (a verb? a canvas? the future? sheer mystery?) then it sounds as if anything goes!

Granted that God is not an object. Granted that he cannot be grasped by reason. Granted that all our thoughts and ideas are quite inadequate. Yet the fact remains that reason, thoughts, words and ideas are all we've got to work with!

And if good reasons cannot be produced, why should one take 'faith' seriously? If faith is to be something more than a mere matter of taste, if it is not to be lumped together with any eccentricity or superstition or sheer delusion, then criteria must be agreed and arguments given.

The objection is a good one. The only adequate reply is of course that the non-believer faces exactly the same quandary! To say that only what can be tested, proved or verified is real, is itself a matter of faith, which cannot be proved.

> *Even reason is a matter of faith. It is an act of faith to assert that our thoughts have any relationship to reality at all.*
> G. K. Chesterton (1874–1936), *Orthodoxy*

So, once again, we reach the conclusion that belief in God is a free choice, which we have to make for ourselves. No one can make it for us.

SAMPLE EXAM QUESTIONS

1 Can God be both righteous and loving?

(UCLES 1990)

2 Is it possible for God to suffer?

(UCLES 1990)

3 'If God knows everything, everything I do is predetermined.' Discuss.

(UCLES 1991)

4 'Your God is too small.' In what ways might a Christian today respond to this challenge?

(UCLES 1992)

5 What are the problems associated with God's omnipotence?

(UCLES 1993)

6 For what reasons do Christians claim 'God is love'?

(UCLES 1994)

4 God and religious experience

Among the proofs for the existence of God, the argument from religious experience (in a vision, a conversion, a message received, etc.) is in a class of its own. A God who is actually *experienced* is no longer something simply abstract – the conclusion of a reasoned argument. God has then become concrete, directly and personally 'seen', 'heard' and 'felt'. A research unit, set up in Oxford since the 1970s, and confirmed by studies at Nottingham University in the 1990s, has concluded that this kind of experience is widespread. Over 60 per cent of the people interviewed claim to have had some sort of significant religious experience, though rarely in the context of organized religion.

All religious experience involves a sense of 'the holy'. In this context, holy does not mean pious, devout, virtuous. It refers to something far more powerful – the awesome, the unspeakable, the utterly different which is felt as both dangerous and attractive at the same time (in Latin: *mysterium tremendum et fascinans*) (see page 25). Many peoples and cultures, high and low and throughout history, have borne witness to this sense of the holy. Millions have claimed that they have met God, not as an abstract 'It' (an object of thought), but as a 'Thou', a subject, sacred and inviolable.

This meeting can offer no proof. It is simply self-authenticating, like the experience of music, or of love. Yet it creates an inner conviction far stronger than any rational argument or proof. And the fact that it is rarely claimed as a private gratification or consolation, but usually issued in a message for all hearers ('Go tell everyone') may suggest that it is something more than wish-fulfilment (see page 43).

EXAMPLES OF RELIGIOUS EXPERIENCE

Abraham, a farmer in Palestine, about 1800 BCE

God tested Abraham and said to him ... 'Take your son, your only son Isaac, whom you love, and go to the land of Moriah, and offer him there as a burnt offering' ... So Abraham cut the wood for the burnt offering, and arose and went to the place of which God had told him ... And Abraham took the wood of the burnt offering, and laid it on Isaac his son; and he took in his hand the fire and the knife. So they went both of them together. And Isaac said to his father ... 'Behold the fire and the wood; but where is the lamb for a burnt offering?' Abraham said, 'God will provide' ...

Abraham built an altar, and laid the wood in order, and bound Isaac his son, and laid him on the altar, upon the wood. Then Abraham put forth his hand, and took the knife to slay his son. But the angel of the Lord called to him from heaven ... 'Do not lay your hand on the lad or do anything to him; for now I know that you fear God.' ... Abraham went and took a ram and offered it up as a burnt offering instead of his son.

Genesis 22: 1–13

Moses, a shepherd in Egypt, about 1300 BCE

The angel of the Lord appeared to Moses in a flame of fire out of the midst of a bush... God called to him out of the bush, 'Do not come near; put off your shoes from your feet, for the place on which you are standing is holy ground'... And Moses hid his face, for he was afraid to look at God... Then the Lord said, 'I will send you to Pharaoh that you may bring forth my people, the sons of Israel, out of Egypt.'

Exodus 3: 2–11

Isaiah, a court prophet in Jerusalem, about 740 BCE

I saw the Lord sitting upon a throne, high and lifted up, and his train filled the Temple. Above him stood the Seraphim... and one called to another and said: 'Holy, holy, holy is the Lord of hosts; the whole earth is full of his glory.' And the foundations of the threshold shook at the voice of him who called, and the Temple was filled with smoke. And I said, 'Woe is me! For I am a man of unclean lips... and my eyes have seen the King, the Lord of hosts!'... And I heard the voice of the Lord saying,... 'Go, and say to this people...'

Isaiah 6: 1–9

Ezekiel, a Jewish exile in Babylon, about 600 BCE

The heavens were opened and I saw visions of God... A stormy wind came out of the north, and a great cloud, with brightness round about it, and fire flashing forth continually... and from the midst of it came the likeness of four living creatures... In the midst of the living creatures there was something that looked like burning coals of fire, like torches moving to and fro, and the fire was bright, and out of the fire went forth lightning... And over their heads there was the likeness of a throne, in appearance like sapphire, and seated above the likeness of a throne was a likeness as it were of a Human Form... Such was the appearance

of the likeness of the glory of the Lord. And when I saw it, I fell upon my face, and I heard the voice of one speaking... 'Son of man, I send you to the people of Israel.'

Ezekiel 1: 1–2: 3

Mary, an unmarried girl in Galilee, 1 CE

The angel Gabriel was sent from God to a city of Galilee named Nazareth, to a young woman betrothed to a man named Joseph... He said, 'Hail, O favoured one, the Lord is with you!' But she was greatly troubled at the saying, and considered in her mind what sort of greeting this might be. And the angel said to her, 'Do not be afraid, Mary, for you have found favour with God. And behold you will conceive in your womb and bear a son, and you shall call his name Jesus.'... And Mary said, 'Behold, I am the handmaid of the Lord, let it be to me according to your word.'

Luke 1: 26–37

Baptism of Jesus

Jesus, at the River Jordan, 27 CE

When Jesus had been baptized and was praying, the heaven was opened, and the Holy Spirit descended upon him in bodily form as a dove, and a voice came from heaven, 'Thou art my beloved Son; with thee I am well pleased.'... And Jesus, full of the Holy Spirit, returned from the Jordan, and was led by the Spirit.

Luke 3: 21–4: 2

Saul, a persecutor of Christians in Palestine, 35 CE

Saul, still breathing threats and murder against the disciples of the Lord, went to the high priest and asked him for letters to the synagogues at Damascus, so that if he found any belonging to the (Christian) Way, he might bring them bound to Jerusalem. Now as he journeyed he approached Damascus, and suddenly a light from heaven flashed about him. And he fell to the ground and heard a voice saying to him, 'Saul, Saul, why do you persecute me?' And he said, 'Who are you, Lord?' And the Lord said, 'I am Jesus, whom you are persecuting; but rise and enter the city, and you will be told what you are to do.'

The Acts of the Apostles 9: 1–6

Muhammad, a trader in Mecca, 610 CE

The Chosen One was praying in a cave on Mt Hira, when a dazzling vision of beauty and light overpowered him, and he heard the word, 'Proclaim!' The Angel Gabriel embraced him and repeated three times, 'Proclaim!' For a moment his soul was filled with divine ecstasy. When he came to, he felt dazed, perplexed and lonely. He spoke of his momentary sense of exaltation, and of the dark void when the curtain fell.

Introduction to the Our'an, 29–31

Mother Julian, a hermit in Norwich, 1373

This is a Revelation of Love that Jesu Christ, our endless blisse, made in xvi shewings...

This Revelation was made to a simple creature, unlettered, living in deadlie flesh, the year of our Lord, a thousand three hundreth lxxiij, the xiiith daie of Maie...

He shewed a little thing, the quantitie of a hazel-nut, lying in the palme of my hand, as me seemed; and it was as round as a ball. I looked thereon with the eie of my understanding, and thought, 'What may this be?' and it was answered generallie thus: 'It is all that is made.' I marveled how it might last: for me thought it might sodenlie have fallen to naught for litleness. And I was answered in my understanding, 'It lasteth and ever shall, for God loveth it. And so hath all thing being by the love of God.'

Revelation of Divine Love,
chapters 1, 2 and 5

Blaise Pascal, French philosopher, 1654

From about half past ten in the evening until half past midnight.
Fire.
God of Abraham, God of Isaac, God of Jacob, not of the philosophers and scholars. Certainty, certainty, heartfelt, joy, peace. God of Jesus Christ...
The world forgotten, and everything except God...
Joy, joy, joy, tears of joy.

Pensées

John Wesley, founder of Methodism, London, 1738

In the evening I went very unwillingly to a society in Aldersgate Street, where one was reading Luther's preface to the Epistle to the Romans. About a quarter before nine, while he was describing the change which God works in the heart through faith in Christ, I felt my heart strangely warmed. I felt I did trust in Christ, Christ alone, for salvation; and an assurance was given me, that he had taken away my sins, even mine, and saved me from the law of sin and death.

Quoted from W. Raeper,
Beginner's Guide to Ideas

C. S. Lewis, university don, Oxford, 1929

You must picture me alone in that room in Magdalen (College), night after night, feeling, whenever my mind lifted even for a second from my work, the steady, unrelenting approach of him whom I most earnestly desired not to meet. That which I so greatly feared had at last come upon me. In the Trinity Term of 1929 I gave in, and admitted that God was God, knelt, and prayed; perhaps, that night, the most dejected and reluctant convert in all England.

Quoted from W. Raeper,
Beginner's Guide to Ideas

Anthony Bloom, an atheist doctor in Paris, 1942

(A priest had been invited to speak to his youth organization.)

When the lecture was over, I hurried home in order to check the truth of what he had been saying. I asked my mother whether she had a book of the Gospel... I started to read St Mark... Before I had reached the third chapter, I suddenly became aware that on the other side of my desk there was a presence. And the certainty was so strong that it was Christ standing there that it has never left me... The Gospel did not unfold for me as a story which one can believe or disbelieve. It began as an event that left all the problems of disbelief behind because it was a direct and personal experience.

School for Prayer

Carlo Carretto, village school teacher, Italy 1944

God's call is mysterious; it comes in the darkness of faith. It is so fine, so subtle, that it is only with the deepest silence within us that we can hear it... This call is uninterrupted: God is always calling us. But there are distinctive moments in this call of his, moments which leave a permanent mark on us... One of these brought about my conversion when I was eighteen years old. I was a school-teacher in a country village. In Lent a mission came to the town. I attended it but what I remember most of all was how boring and outdated the sermons were... But when I knelt before the old missionary – I remember how direct his look was and how simple – I was aware that God was moving in the silence of my soul. From that day on I knew I was a Christian.

Letters from the Desert

Catriona Devereux, on a skiing holiday, Geneva, 1993

(Her brother Sean, a 28-year-old volunteer teaching in a Christian school in Africa, was assassinated during the civil war in Somalia in 1993.)

Just before I heard the news of Sean's death, I was sitting alone in this ski chalet in Geneva. The classical music was playing, and they've got a beautiful, beautiful window overlooking the mountains, and I just had this most fantastic feeling of love and expansion – it was just really weird, I never experienced it before, it was just kind of like, just complete, just love and completeness, it was really weird. And I thought, 'God! What's wrong with me?' – I just felt so odd! And then I heard the news. It was an immense shock really. I was standing by the telephone, and I just buckled over, it was just really awful. But then that feeling of kind of love and expansion, it came again at the funeral, and also when I actually saw Sean's body. And I haven't had it since then. So it's really weird. But it was a wonderful feeling.

Television interview, *Everyman*

These quotations speak of fairly dramatic experiences. Many religious traditions bear similar witness. And not only of making contact with a 'numinous' or awe-inspiring world beyond our own, but of actually being drawn into that world, and somehow becoming one with it.

This mystical experience goes beyond an awareness of God, and becomes a lost absorption into God, in which the self is totally lost in a union with God so ecstatic that it is literally unspeakable. Hinduism bears witness to this mystical experience among its devotees of *Bhakti*, Islam in its contemplative *Sufis*, Judaism in its joy-filled *Kabbalists* and *Hasidim*, and Christianity in mystics like St John of the Cross and St Teresa of Avila.

It goes without saying that not all religious experience is as spectacular as this. Nor does it need to be. Believers would claim that the experience of anything at depth (goodness, beauty, love, forgiveness, grief, bereavement) – and even more the experience of being confronted, challenged, addressed, and summoned to respond by changing one's life – this is genuinely religious experience even when it is not given that name. 'God' is the word believers use to point to those depths.

THE EXPERIENCE OF PRAYER

One of the arguments frequently put forward for the existence of God is the experience many have had of their prayers to God being answered. How good an argument is this?

Escapism?

If there is a God, then it seems reasonable to address him in praise, in humble confession, or in thanksgiving. But in what sense can it be reasonable to ask God to provide the things people need? Is not such an exercise a form of escapism, an attempt to offload the responsibilities that people ought to be shouldering themselves? Is there not a danger of such a practice keeping humans in a perpetual state of infancy? Should not a humanity that has 'come of age' dispense with an activity that belongs to its childish past?

There is a deeper difficulty still. Such a practice seems unworthy not only of an adult human race, but of God himself. Is God to be imagined to be willing to bestow his goods (health, wealth, sustenance, safety, etc.) only if he is asked? Is he to be thought of as changing his mind in response to prayer? Does he give daily bread to all who ask, so that those who do not receive must be judged to be in his bad books?

One could put the difficulty even more pungently. Is not the God who stands hidden behind most people's understanding of intercessory prayer utterly immoral, let alone unworthy? Taken to its logical conclusion, prayer of this kind is an attempt to put pressure on God. It assumes that, given a formula which is appropriate, God can be bribed or blackmailed, manoeuvred or manipulated, coaxed, cajoled or controlled. And a God of this kind many people find so abhorrent that they can no longer accept him. Prayer presupposes a God who is not God-like enough.

Jesus' teaching

The fact is, of course, that even if the Bible with its picture language sometimes portrays God in childlike terms, its actual positive teaching (especially in the ministry of Jesus) is designed to undermine an infantile understanding of God. For Jesus, the kingdom or rule of God is not 'in the hands of the gods', but can be brought about only by human beings. God is not the Supreme Outsider who now and again intervenes in human affairs. He is the Supreme Insider, living in people's hearts, and freeing them to be themselves and to create their own future.

In short, the message of Christianity is that God has handed over the world to the human race and confidently expects it to cope. In praying, people accept the responsibility for God's business as theirs. When they stand before God in an attitude of prayer, they are acknowledging that all they do is based in him and is done in the hope of manifesting him. Prayer is simply one of the ways in which they show concern for the world they live in.

Why continue to ask?

It could be objected that a God who does not intervene miraculously for his friends, but expects them to assume responsibility for themselves and to take charge of their own world, sounds dangerously like no God at all. Why turn to such a God in prayer?

Could it be that there is some other purpose for praying, distinct from having the prayer answered by an outside agency? Perhaps. The prayer may serve a therapeutic purpose for example, in giving voice to a need. And indeed, unless there are people who cry out in protest against things that are plainly evil, even against impossible odds, even when the prayer is apparently not 'answered', there is nothing to prevent the final triumph of evil.

There are cases where the very act of praying is the first step towards people doing something about the matter themselves. There are cases where what is prayed for is already granted by being verbalized: anyone who has enemies can wondrously change them into allies by the simple expedient of praying for them; those who pray for peace have already begun the process whereby peace will be brought about.

And finally there are cases where prayer is answered because people believe that the God to whom they pray is present among them as the love which binds them together. If God is love, then the most normal way in which he answers the prayers of those in need is through the loving concern of their brothers and sisters. That loving concern *is* the presence and action of God. If such prayers are not answered, it is because there is insufficient love. One could say that God has not answered these prayers because the lack of love has crippled his presence in the community.

Serving God is doing good to others but praying for them is thought an easier service, and therefore is more generally chosen.

Benjamin Franklin, 1706–1790

The purpose of prayer

All the cases referred to above suggest that the purpose of intercessory prayer is not (as is often thought) to change God, but to change the interceder. This is the conclusion arrived at long ago by the medieval philosopher Thomas Aquinas:

Petitions made to other people are not based on the same need as petitions made to God. A petition made to a man tells him of the petitioner's desire or need, and hopes to move him to do something about it. This is not true of petitions addressed to God. He knows our need and desires. Nor can he be moved by human words to do what previously was against his will.

Petitionary prayer to God is necessary to man. It influences the petitioner. It makes him realize his own weakness, and ardently desire what he prays for. In this way he makes himself capable of attaining it.

Compendium Theologiae II, 2

Former Chief Rabbi (now Lord) Jakobovits agrees:

God knows what is in me – I don't need to tell him. So I recite prayers to impress a certain message on myself – my dependence on God. For I am the addressee. The form of the prayer is addressed to God, but I'm not meant to change God, I'm meant to change myself... God's response to my prayer is that I seek to become a nobler being.

The Times, 1987

Conclusion

If prayer, understood in this sense, continues to be expressed in terms of 'asking', it is not necessarily because some *outside* agency is expected miraculously to grant the request. It could be that everything needing to be done has to be done by people themselves. They 'ask' simply because they need again and again to acknowledge that they are totally rooted in and dependent on God. Everything is a gift, even the human power to change the world. That indebtedness is acknowledged by asking even for the things that are most taken for granted, like light and air and sunshine.

People's prayer of intercession is answered by God when they work with the God who is both with them and for them, to bring about what is being prayed for.

I saw that the only way that God could take a hand in tragedy was through us, me included, because we were the only hands he'd got. And his only power, as Simone Weil said, was the love he inspired in us – there was nothing else to offer... 'Why doesn't God take a hand in it?' became 'Why don't I take a hand in it?' and this made sense. I don't like misusing prayer to avoid realism.

Rabbi Lionel Blue, *The Tablet,* 1996

For discussion
What do you think happens when people pray for victims of famine or drought or war?

THE EXPERIENCE OF REVELATION

Revelation means the unveiling of something that was previously hidden. In the present context, it refers to God's disclosure of himself to people.

There is a sense in which revelation is the most ordinary thing in the world. A God who is the creator of all things cannot help being revealed (as any artist is) in what he has created. The whole world is, as it were, a visible and tangible embodiment of the invisible and intangible God. There must be 'that of God' in everything and in everyone – like father like son. God has always been present in the flesh (in-carnation) of all things, and revealed in every blade of grass.

The sky proclaims God's glory,
its dome his handicraft:
day to following day,
night to following night
tells his story.

Psalm 19: 1–2

God's voice sounds over the great waters,
the glorious God thunders!
God over the great waters!
God's strong voice
God's majestic voice!
God's voice shattering the cedars...
God's voice shakes the desert!
God's voice sets the oak trees whirling
and strips the forest bare!
In his temple everything cries 'Glory!'

Psalm 29: 3–9
translated by Alan Dale, *Winding Quest*

For believers, therefore, there is a sense in which revelation is the most ordinary thing in the world. Perhaps it is misleading to make a hard and fast distinction between the *natural* knowledge of God which we arrive at under our own steam, and the *supernatural* knowledge which we need God to reveal to us. There is a sense in which *all* knowledge of God, even what we call 'natural', is a gift, an amazing grace.

In other words, however 'chosen' or 'privileged' any group may claim to be, God would, in this case, have to be seen as speaking and revealing himself at all times to all people. This presence of God to everyone and everything is more important than any particular group's feeling of specialness.

'Are you not like the Ethiopians to me,
O people of Israel?' says the Lord.
'Did I not bring up Israel from the land of
Egypt,

> *and the Philistines from Crete,*
> *and the Syrians from Mesopotamia?'*
>
> Amos 9: 7
>
> *There has never been a time*
> *when God has not told people that he loves*
> *them.*
> *Right from the beginning,*
> *and through all the ages,*
> *that is what he has told all people*
> *everywhere.*
> *But not all people have understood what*
> *God was telling them,*
> *even when God was saying, in so many*
> *words,*
> *'Come and be members of my family.'*
> *So this Word of God became human,*
> *and lived a human life like ours,*
> *so that we could touch and feel what God*
> *was telling us.*
> *The Word was made flesh and dwelt*
> *amongst us.*
> *In him we see the God who can't be seen.*
>
> John 1: 1–18 translated by H. J. Richards

This having been said, it remains obvious that some experiences of God (for example, those referred to at the beginning of this chapter, pp 35–38) go beyond this general sense of God's presence in all things. It is with this extraordinary and particular kind of revelation that we will be dealing in what follows.

Prophecy and miracles

Is there any way of verifying this alleged religious experience? How can we distinguish between a genuine revelation from God and a mere human delusion? How can we tell a true spokesperson for God from a false one? What criteria should we use to decide? Once upon a time, comets and eclipses (and even the rainbow itself – see Genesis 9:13) were seen as supernatural messages sent by God; they are now seen as entirely natural events. Will all claims to special divine revelation eventually evaporate in the same way?

Prophecy is often offered as proof. The future is known only to God. Anyone who accurately foretells the future is a man of God, and has God's authorization for everything he says.

But there are snags to such a solution.

- Even in the Bible, such foretellings are rare. In particular, the texts often referred to as 'Old Testament' prophecies of the New Testament' turn out to be idealized hopes, rather than actual predictions.
- How can we distinguish between a real foretelling of the future and a shrewdly accurate guess (e.g. the Fall of Jerusalem in 70 CE, apparently foretold by Jesus according to the Gospels)?
- What use is a prediction that cannot be verified for centuries?

Miracles are also traditionally proposed as a proof that one is speaking on behalf of God, who alone can give people the power to perform such marvellous works. But here too there are snags.

- It is often impossible (especially in ancient literature) to determine what precisely took place. Are the stories exaggerated? Or symbolic rather than factual?
- Both Jewish and Christian traditions speak of rival miracles being performed by people opposed to God (see the box below). So what do those miracles prove?
- In the Muslim tradition, 'the miraculous' is almost totally ignored. Muhammad himself claimed no miraculous powers.
- Healings in particular, however 'miraculous', tend to be understood today in natural or psychosomatic terms. This does not exclude God, but neither does it prove he has intervened.
- See also chapter 7, pages 84–91.

> *The Lord said to Moses, 'When Pharaoh*
> *says to you, "Prove yourselves by working a*
> *miracle", say to Aaron, "Take your rod and*
> *cast it down before Pharaoh so that it may*

become a serpent"' ... And it became a serpent. Then Pharaoh summoned ... the magicians of Egypt, and they did the same by their secret arts ... Moses and Aaron struck the Nile and all the water was turned to blood...But the magicians of Egypt did the same...Aaron stretched out his hand over the waters of Egypt, and the frogs came up and covered the land of Egypt. But the magicians did the same.

Exodus 7: 8–8: 7

False Christs and false prophets will arise and show great signs and wonders, so as to lead astray, if possible, even the elect.

Matthew 24: 24

The coming of the Lawless One, by the activity of Satan, will be with all power and pretended signs and wonders.

2 Thessalonians 2: 9

The Beast works great signs, even making fire come down from heaven to earth...to deceive those who dwell on earth.

Revelation 13: 13–14

In the light of texts like these, it is interesting that the Bible, which otherwise shows great reverence for prophecy and miracles, finally rejects both as knock-down proofs of divine intervention. As the Israelites take over Palestine to make it their own, Moses is represented as making this ruling:

If a prophet arises among you
and gives you a sign or wonder (miracle),
even if the sign or wonder comes to pass
*   (prophecy),*
and if he says, 'Let us go after other gods',
you shall not listen to the words of that prophet;
the Lord your God is testing you ...
That prophet shall be put to death,
because he has taught rebellion against the
*   Lord your God ...*
your hand shall be the first against him to
*   put him to death.*

Deuteronomy 13: 1–9

In other words, an experience of God is proved to be true, not by supernatural fireworks, but by its coherence with what else we have already experienced of God. I can recognize something as being 'of God' when it is consistent with, and deepens, 'that of God' which is already in me.

Conclusion

In conclusion, it would therefore seem that there is no cast-iron proof that God reveals himself. Yet it is not unreasonable to presume that, if there *is* a God, he would make himself known to his creation. This revelation does not need to be authenticated externally. It is self-authenticating, but cannot be proved, only believed. In this, of course, it is just like atheism itself! (See also pages 33, 48, 68).

Robert *What did you mean when you said that St Catherine and St Margaret talked to you every day?*
Joan of Arc *They do.*
Robert *What are they like?*
Joan (suddenly obstinate) *I will tell you nothing about that: they have not given me leave.*
Robert *But you actually see them; and they talk to you just as I am talking to you?*
Joan *No: it is quite different. I cannot tell you; you must not talk to me about my voices.*
Robert *How do you mean? Voices?*
Joan *I hear voices telling me what to do. They come from God.*
Robert *They come from your imagina tion.*
Joan *Of course. That is how the messages of God come to us.*

George Bernard Shaw, *Saint Joan* II, 1

Jean Seberg in the film *St Joan*

For discussion

Do you feel that Shaw, in the passage above, is cheating, or making a very good point?

Your companion Muhammad does not err, nor does he speak of his own will. It is nothing other than a revelation that has been revealed to him.

Surah 53

A rabbinical story tells of a man who wandered from village to village asking, 'Where can I find God?' In some places he was told to pray, but he could not find God there. In other places they told him to study, but this only confused him the more. Elsewhere he was told that God was within him but he could not find him there.

Eventually he arrived at a place where he asked a woman tending the chickens where he could find God. Expressing no surprise, she sent him to the rabbi, who said, 'You have come to the right place: God is in this village.'

He decided to stay. When he asked the villagers who God was, they smiled and asked him in for a meal. Gradually he got to know them all, and helped with the village work, and over the years became part of the community. And he was never sure where or when God was to be found, but also knew that sometimes he had found him.

One day the rabbi asked him, 'Well have you found God now?' He replied that he had, but could not say how or why. The rabbi said, 'God is not a person or a thing that you can meet. When you came here, you were looking for something that wasn't God at all, and so you couldn't find him. But now that you've stopped persecuting God, you've found him, and you can go home if you wish.'

So he went back to his town, and God went with him. And when people asked him, 'Where can we find God?' he would answer, 'You've come to the right spot: God is in this place.'

For discussion

How would you go about convincing someone that God had spoken to you?

What exactly is the difference between saying 'God spoke to me in a dream', and saying 'I dreamt God spoke to me'? Is one more real than the other?

REVELATION AND SCRIPTURE ▬▬▬▬

Sacred books

For most believers, revelation has little to do with any personal experience of their own. Revelation, for them, more usually refers to an event or events in the distant past in which God is said to have revealed himself, and of which a permanent record has been preserved in their 'sacred writings' or scriptures, through which God is still said to 'speak'.

Most religious groups have such a collection of writing venerated as the 'Word of God': Jews with their Mosaic Torah and the Prophets, Christians with their Gospels and Epistles, Hindus with their Vedas,

Muslims with their Qur'an, the Latter Day Saints with their Book of Mormon, etc.

Disagreement

Since these various 'revelations' disagree with each other on some fairly fundamental points, it is difficult to accept them all as the Word of God. Since all of them, in their own way, claim to speak the last word, a choice must presumably be made between them. But on what grounds?

Worse still, even in the same one Christian Bible, there are different ways of understanding the text (which cannot interpret itself). Which interpretation is the right one? Disagreement on this question first divided Christians from Jews, and then split eastern Christians from western, Catholics from Protestants, and finally each of a dozen Protestant denominations from each other.

Literally or critically?

Even so, the deepest split remains between those, of whatever denomination, who insist that the text must be understood as literally and absolutely as possible (**Literalism**), and those, again of whatever denomination, who insist on subjecting the text to the kind of textual, literary and historical critique which one would apply to any literature. The word 'criticism' in this context does not mean finding fault, but asking searching questions.

The word **Fundamentalism** is often used as if it were synonymous with Literalism. In fact it is a far more flexible movement, based on the perceived need to defend the 'fundamentals' of Christianity against excessive biblical criticism. Fundamentalists fear that the advance of science could extinguish Christianity altogether unless doctrines are rigidly defined, barriers erected and laws stringently observed. This does not necessarily require a literalist understanding of the Bible.

It is, of course, not only Christians who have had to rethink their understanding of their sacred books, but Jews and Muslims too. 'Orthodox' Jews generally continue to insist on a rigorously literal interpretation of the Bible, whatever difficulties modern science throws in their path. But an increasing number of Jews in the last two centuries have felt the need to adjust their understanding of their sacred books to the findings of science, and have moved away from Orthodoxy to found the *Reformed* and *Liberal* movements. These continue to pay the utmost respect to the Bible as the foundation of Judaism, but interpret it in a far less rigid way.

Revelation is not the communication of infallible information, nor the outpouring of 'inspired' sages and poets . . . It is the self-disclosure of God in his dealings with the world. Scripture is a story composed of many strands and fragments . . . it is the story of the encounter of God with man in the history of Israel.

W. Herberg, *Judaism and Modern Man*, Jewish Publication Society of America (quoted in *Judaism*, Heinemann, p. 142)

As for Muslims, for whom the Qur'an is so 'heaven-sent' that no translation of it can be regarded as anything more than a clumsy paraphrase, this sacred book too has not always been interpreted in a fundamentalist way. The great Muslim philosophers of medieval times found no conflict between their faith and a genuinely scientific study of the world in which they lived (see page 15). And in spite of the Islamic backlash against 'modernization' in many countries, there are others which have seen a radical adaptation of the Qur'an to the secular world in which we live today.

Among Christians too, disagreement about the interpretation of their sacred books runs deep. Readers on both sides of the divide refer to the Bible as 'God's Word', but they understand this in quite different ways. For some, the Bible cannot be God's revelation unless it is dictated by him word for word. What the Bible says is final, and to pose difficulties is to question God's authority. Others prefer to start from the fact that the Bible is obviously a thoroughly human book, with all the quirks and foibles that are to be found in any human literature. Only when this is accepted is it appropriate, they feel, to ask the question: 'How can such a thoroughly human work be referred to as the Word of God?'.

The Bible as a human book

Any random selection of excerpts would confirm that, whatever else the Bible is, it is first of all a collection of fallible (limited, provisional, sometimes banal) words of fallible human beings. Moreover, these excerpts are not all of a kind. There are pages of straight history and legislation, but these are placed alongside essays, diaries, story books, prayers and letters. There are sermons and serious theological articles, but they rub shoulders with love poems and songs. Clearly all these were not designed to be read in the same tone of voice. Each piece must be read in the 'key' (or *literary form*) intended by the author, or there will be disharmony. A piece intended as fiction should not be taken as fact. Expert help is needed to decide which is which.

Being written in an unscientific age, the Bible frequently makes errors about cosmological, geographical, historical, archaeological, etc., facts. But then so did everyone else. It would be foolish to imagine that these errors have God's seal of approval simply because they are in the Bible. The biblical authors were not concerned with the *how?* or *when?* or *where?* of the human race. They were concerned with the deeper questions of *who?* and *why?* As Galileo had already observed in his time, the Scriptures were not given to us to show us how the heavens go, but how to go to heaven.

The fact that the Bible is concerned with the 'deeper questions' means that none of its stories (some are even told two or three times, with variations) is told for its own sake. The stories are told only for the sake of their *meaning*. All of them are typical of people who prefer to say what they have to say in a dramatic and concrete way ('Let me tell you a story') rather than in the abstract. This means that until the meaning of the story (even of the factual one) has come across, we misunderstand it. The stories of Adam and Eve or of David and Solomon, or of the Good Samaritan, are not told to provide information. Nor are they proved true when people can point to the actual spot where they took place. They are true when people can see the deep meaning of the stories for themselves.

Only when this thoroughly human nature of the Bible is acknowledged can its divine nature be faced with honesty. How can something so human be called the inspired Word of God ('breathed out' by God)?

The Bible as the Word of God

It needs to be stated that 'Word of God' is a metaphor – God does not literally have a voice. Nor is his activity exclusive, like human activity, where what is done by *A* is not done by *B*. God does not act *instead* of people, but always in and through them.

It also needs to be repeated that, whatever else 'Word of God' means, it cannot mean that the Bible is dictated by God, or contains no errors. Nor may it be turned into an absolute – only God is absolute.

God speaks to the world not through a divine loudspeaker out of heaven, but through sources close to him. These sources (Moses, David, Paul, Jesus, and others) cannot answer our questions directly; they can only tell us how, living in their times, they saw their relationship with God. But when what God 'spoke' to them is reflected into the lives we live in *our* times, then God can be said to 'speak' to us too.

In this way, God has always 'spoken' to the human race, and his Word has been heard by people who have never come across any 'Holy Scriptures'.

> *In the beginning was the Word...*
> *Its life was the light of man...*
> *giving light to everyone...*
> *and the power to become children of God.*
>
> John 1: 1–12
>
> *Imagine a sower going out to sow...*
> *Some seeds fell into rich soil,*
> *grew tall and strong,*
> *and produced a good crop;*
> *the yield was thirty, sixty, even a*
> *hundredfold...*
> *What the sower is sowing is the Word.*
>
> Mark 4: 3–14, *New Jerusalem Bible*

Why, then, should the Bible be necessary? The answer is that, for Christians, the New Testament is the irreplaceable record of how people had experienced God speaking definitively in the life of Jesus. And this same Jesus had based his entire life on the Old Testament, where *he* had first found God. Christians have always felt the need to reflect with Jesus on these rich pages which describe the journey of faith which Jesus' own people (the Jews) had to make throughout their long history.

Both Jesus and the Bible have been given the title 'Word of God'. In the case of Jesus, this does not mean that he was a man excluding God, nor God excluding man, nor half of one and half of the other. He was the whole truth about God, lived out in the life of an ordinary human being.

The Bible, too, cannot be regarded as simply another piece of human literature, nor as a divine broadcast from heaven, nor as sometimes one and sometimes the other. For Christians, the Bible is the whole truth about God, expressed in ordinary human (and therefore inadequate) terms. It does not *contain* God's Word like a carrier bag, but rather *becomes* God's Word as the

authors say to the reader, 'This is how I see God. How do you see him?' And in the interaction between the author's witness and the reader's understanding, God is again present, and speaks.

> *Break thou the bread of life,*
> *O Lord, to me,*
> *As thou didst break the loaves,*
> *Beside the sea;*
> *Beyond the sacred page*
> *I seek thee, Lord;*
> *My spirit pants for thee,*
> *O living Word.*
>
> Mary Lathbury (1841–1913)
> *Methodist Hymn Book*

For discussion
Does this analysis of the Bible make it too human for your liking? Or too divine?

How convincing is the argument for the existence of God from religious experience?

In this chapter we have looked at a great variety of forms of religious experience (visions, heavenly voices, conversions, vocations, answered prayers, divine revelation, etc.) and considered the final crystallization of some of this experience in writings now venerated as inspired Scripture. How should this vast amount of material be judged? Does it prove the existence of God any more convincingly than the arguments we considered in chapter 2? Has God (if there is one) really revealed himself in these varied experiences?

The question needs to be asked not only in reference to private experiences such as those listed on pages 35–38, but also in reference to the group experiences of which examples may be found in every age of human history. The 'Toronto Blessing' of the late 1990s is only the most recent example, where group ecstasy and rapture have been experienced as an outpouring of God's Spirit so spectacular that within a few years it has spread to centres throughout the world, arousing considerable opposition from mainstream Christian churches. How genuinely are such experiences rooted in God?

It is not easy to tell. After all, the Muslim movement, not to mention the original Jesus movement, aroused considerable opposition at their first showing. It is obvious that the person who has a religious experience does not need proof that it is real, yet while it is equally obvious that the sceptic does! How can anyone ever be sure that these 'experiences' are not delusions, self-induced wish-fulfilments? They are claimed to be real and objective, but is there any way of verifying this? Could they perhaps be nothing more than psychotic fantasies, revealing a childish need of a father figure and a neurotic refusal to grow up? (This is the 'solution' offered by Sigmund Freud – see page 74.) Will not science (especially the science of psychology) eventually dispel this 'supernatural' area, just as it has eliminated God from any explanation of eclipses and earthquakes? (the suggestion of Karl Marx – see page **73**).

Such scepticism is not new. Even the Hebrew Bible is concerned about the possibility of delusion or even deception in this matter. How can we distinguish someone who genuinely speaks on behalf of God (a prophet) from the fraud? By the ability to perform miracles? Or to foretell the future? The Jewish book of Deuteronomy repudiates these apparently simple criteria.

The prophet who presumes to speak a word in my name which I have not commanded him to speak... shall die. And if you say in your heart, 'How may we know the word which the Lord has not spoken?' – when a prophet speaks in the name of the Lord, if the word (foretelling the future) does not

come to pass, that is a word which the Lord has not spoken...

(However) if a prophet arises among you and gives you a sign or a wonder, (even if) the sign or wonder which he tells you comes to pass, if he then says, 'Let us go after other gods and serve them', you shall not listen to the words of that prophet... he shall be put to death.

Deuteronomy 18: 20–22, 13: 1–5

The text states unhesitatingly that it is possible to tell whether people have a genuine experience of God: not by their ability to perform wonders or foretell the future, but by the consistency of their message. Does the God who shows himself in this religious experience tie in with the God who has made himself known in other religious experiences? The criterion is, of course, far more difficult to apply, even though it is the one which the Christian Gospels invite their readers to use for judging Jesus: 'Who do you say that I am?'

To conclude, religious experience is perhaps the most powerful of all arguments for the existence of God ('Stop trying to tell me God does not exist – I've *met* him!'). Even so, like the other arguments, it is not finally convincing except to those who have actually had the experience, since other explanations of the experience cannot automatically be excluded.

But this may not be used as an argument *against* the existence of God. The fact that some religious experiences may be illusory does not mean that they all are. The major religions have all borne witness to so many individual instances of religious experience, that it is difficult to dismiss it as something 'merely subjective'. The American philosopher and psychologist William James (see page 73), after years of research, came to the conclusion that if an experience of this kind was short-lasting and indescribable, offered new insights and was not self-induced, it had to be accepted as objective and authentic.

After all, some of the finest and most mature people, giving the most hassle to thought-police throughout history, have claimed to be in touch with God. We must each make up our own mind whether such people were deluded. And the answer 'yes' is as much an act of faith as the answer 'no'.

For discussion

Does belief in God depend totally, or partly, or in no way, on background and upbringing?

SAMPLE EXAM QUESTIONS

1 How useful is religious experience as evidence for the existence of God?

(OCR AS sample paper)

2 How far are liberal interpretations of Scripture influenced by ideas of their time?

(OCR AS and A sample paper)

3 'Claims to religious experience say more about the mental health of the believer than they do about the existence of God.' Discuss.

(OCR A sample paper)

4 To what extent can it be maintained that a literal interpretation of Scripture removes all danger of human error?

(OCR A sample paper)

5 In what sense, if at all, can the Bible be considered to be the inspired Word of God?

(OCR A sample paper)

6 'Psychologists have dealt a fatal blow to those who claim to know from experience that God exists.' Discuss.

(OCR A sample paper) (essay)

5 God and evil

THE PROBLEM

THE human race has always been tormented by the problem of evil and suffering, and all religions have had to cope with the problem. Even in the Bible, it appears on the very first pages, which plaintively ask how a world created totally good could become good-and-evil. It haunts the whole history of Israel, whose frequent failures are listed with disarming honesty. It recurs over and over again in the anguished 'Why?' which punctuates the book of Psalms. It forms the sole topic of discussion in one of the Old Testament's lengthier books, Job. In the New Testament, the story of Jesus is nothing other than the account of his evil suffering and death, with a long introduction. And the theme is still to the forefront in the closing book of the Christian Bible, with the apocalyptic hope that evil will finally be vanquished and eliminated.

The problem is easily put:

> **God is all powerful**
> **God is all loving**
> **Evil exists.**

Of these three propositions, only two seem to be compatible, never all three. That is to say, evil could exist because God is powerful enough to prevent it, but not loving enough to do so. Or evil could exist because God lovingly wishes to prevent it, but is not powerful enough to do so. Or finally, since God is both willing and able to prevent evil, evil cannot exist.

The fact, of course, is that evil *does* exist. How can that be squared with God's power and love? Does not some of the guilt of the evil attach to a God who apparently does nothing about it? And this question can be asked even when we exclude all the evil for which humans are responsible: war, rape, torture, injustice, etc. There still remain all the natural disasters for which presumably only God can be held responsible: earthquakes, volcanic eruptions, drought, famine, disability, sickness and death. Insurance policies call all these 'acts of God'.

SOLUTIONS

THE philosophical attempts to solve the problem of evil have been known, ever since the time of Leibniz (1646–1716), as **Theodicy**, that is, the justification or exoneration (*diké*) of God (*theos*). A number of these are listed below, in no order of merit. There are presumably grains of truth even in the least satisfactory of them.

Atheism

The simplest solution to the problem of evil is to accept the logic of the three incompatible propositions quoted above. An almighty and loving God does not square with the existence of evil. But evil clearly exists. Therefore, equally clearly, God cannot exist.

The universe is not the Garden of Eden depicted in the Bible. It is not even the intricately designed piece of clockwork described by Paley (see page 18), or the perfect billiard table discovered by Newton (see page 70). It is Macbeth's 'tale told by an idiot' – mindless, meaningless, and quite absurd.

I cannot imagine any omnipotent sentient being sufficiently cruel to create the world we inhabit.

Iris Murdoch, *A Severed Head*

If the world which we inhabit has been produced in accordance with a plan, we shall have to reckon Nero a saint in comparison with the Author of that plan. Fortunately, however, the evidence of divine purpose is non-existent. We are, therefore, spared the necessity for that attitude of impotent hatred which every brave and humane man would otherwise be called upon to adopt towards the Almighty Tyrant.

Bertrand Russell (1872–1970)

How are atheists produced? In probably nine cases out of ten, what happens is something like this:

A beloved husband, or wife, or child, or sweetheart is gnawed to death by cancer, stultified by epilepsy, struck dumb and helpless by apoplexy, or strangled by croup or diphtheria; and the looker on, after praying vainly to God to refrain from such horrible and wanton cruelty, indignantly repudiates faith in the divine monster, and becomes not merely indifferent and sceptical, but fiercely and actively hostile to religion.

George Bernard Shaw (1856–1950)

The Eternal replied to Job from the midst of the tempest: 'Did I not create the crocodile which surpasses all the rest in abomination? Cannot the crocodile bite, slaughter, cripple, mutilate, destroy? How can you doubt my authority when I am the master of abominations?'

Then Job replied to the Eternal and said: 'You are right, I recognize that you are the most ignoble, the most repugnant, the most brutal, the most perverse, the most sadistic and the most nauseating being in the world. I recognize that you are a despot and a tyrant and a potentate who obliterates and kills everything... You invented the Gestapo, the concentration camp and

torture; so I recognize that you are the greatest and the strongest. Praised be the name of the Lord!'

F. Zorn quoted in D. Morin,
How to Understand God

In sober truth, nearly all the things which men are hanged or imprisoned for doing to one another are nature's (God's) everyday performances. Killing, the most criminal act recognised by human law, nature does once to every being that lives, and in a large proportion of cases after protracted tortures... Nature impales men, breaks them as if on the wheel, casts them to be devoured by wild beasts, burns them to death, starves them with hunger, freezes them with cold, poisons them... and has hundreds of other hideous deaths in reserve such as the ingenious cruelty of a Domitian never surpassed. All this nature does with the most supercilious disregard both of mercy and of justice... Everything, in short, which the worst men commit either against life or property is perpetrated on a larger scale by nature... Not even on the most distorted and contracted theory of good which was ever framed by religious or philosophical fanaticism can the government of nature resemble the work of a Being at once good and omnipotent.

J. S. Mill (1806–73)
Nature and Utility of Religion

For discussion

Do you see these angry objections as overstatements or understatements?

Dualism

Evil cannot be blamed on God, because it stems from a second almighty principle, an Antigod. It is he that is responsible for evil: only good things come from God. The universe is the battlefield on which the Principle of Good and the Principle of Evil fight for domination. The struggle will continue for all time. The final victory can only come at the end.

This world-view has been shared by many people, even today. It was the view of the Zoroastrians of ancient Persia, according to whom the Lord of Light, Ahura-Mazda, is locked in perpetual combat with his rival, the Lord of Darkness. The neighbours of ancient Israel also shared this view, and they bequeathed much of their imagery to the Bible and to the Qur'an.

Darkness was upon the face of the deep . . . And God said, 'Let there be light.'

Genesis 1: 2

Thou didst divide the sea by thy might, thou didst break the heads of the Dragons on the waters. Thou didst crush the heads of Leviathan.

Psalm 73: 13–14

Through the devil's envy death entered the world.

Wisdom 2: 24

The Lord said to Satan, 'Behold he (Job) is in your power.'

Job 2: 6

Jesus was in the wilderness forty days, tempted by Satan.

Mark 1: 13

A man with an evil spirit cried out, 'What have you to do with us, Jesus of Nazareth? Have you come to destroy us?'

Mark 1: 23

Satan entered into Judas called Iscariot.

Luke 22: 3

We are not contending against flesh and blood, but against Principalities and Powers, World Rulers of this present darkness.

Ephesians 6: 12

In that day the Lord . . . will punish Leviathan . . . He will slay the Dragon that is in the sea.

Isaiah 27: 1

The great Dragon was thrown down, that ancient Serpent who is called the Devil and Satan, the deceiver of the whole world . . . Now the Kingdom of our God has come.

Revelation 12: 9–10

It is Satan who desires to sow enmity and hate among you . . . and to lead you away from remembrance of God and prayer.

Qur'an 5: 94

In a wartime concentration camp, three rabbis put God on trial for the suffering of the Jews. They found him guilty. They added that the only counsel they could have called to speak on God's behalf would have been Satan.

Elie Wiesel, BBC Interview

However, it is important to note that, in spite of this dramatic and polarized imagery, Judaism, Christianity and Islam remain *monistic*, not dualistic. Whatever the word 'Devil' stands for, he is not (whether in Jewish, Christian or Muslim thought) a rival to God, but God's creature and therefore God's responsibility. The oneness of God remains central, however many problems this raises – as in the following texts.

I *will harden Pharaoh's heart.*

Exodus 4: 21; 7: 3; 10: 1; 14: 4, 17

The Lord *hardened the heart of Pharaoh.*

Exodus 9: 12; 10: 20, 27; 11: 10; 14: 8

I form light and *darkness, I make weal* and *create woe, I am the Lord, who do* all *these things.*

Isaiah 45: 7

Shall we receive good at the hand of God, and shall we not receive evil too?

Job 2: 10

Good things and *bad, life* and *death, wealth* and *poverty, come from the Lord.*

Ecclesiasticus 11: 14

I believe in God . . . and believe everything – both good and bad – comes from him.

From the Muslim profession of faith

> **For discussion**
> What do you think about these statements which suggest that 'the Devil' is ultimately God's responsibility?

Evil is unreal

Evil is not something that God has deliberately created. In fact it is not a positive reality at all, but simply a negative absence of good, a deprivation, as in the case, for example, of an eye that is blind instead of seeing, or a leg that has been amputated. In this sense, God cannot be held responsible for evil. Less still, of course, when the positively good things he has created are found in the wrong place: a good strong cancer which has attacked a bone, for example, or an efficient weedkiller

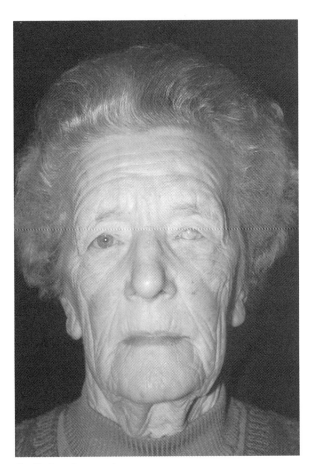

God's hands are clean

which has been put in someone's tea, or an earthquake that takes place where people happen to live. God's hands are clean.

According to this solution of St Augustine (340–430 CE), evil is merely negative, a non-being, an unreality, totally dissociated from God the source of reality. This outlook has some similarity to the teaching of Hinduism and Buddhism, according to which evil is simply an illusion, brought about by human craving and greed. To rebel against it simply makes matters worse. It can be dealt with only by becoming more and more detached, in order to liberate the true self that lies hidden deep beneath our deceptive external selves.

There is perhaps an element of unreality in the claim that evil is unreal! It is a solution that may appeal to the armchair philosopher, but offers little comfort to the person who is actually suffering: someone with cancer, for example, or a bereaved mother. Nor will it ever appeal very strongly to Christians, for whom the problem of evil is epitomized in the death of Jesus.

Original sin

None of the evil in the world, not even so-called 'acts of God', can be blamed on God. All evil originated in the human race's primeval rebellion against God.

A literal reading of the first chapters of Genesis would suggest 'original sin' was preceded by 'original blessing', where the whole of creation is seven times acclaimed as 'good'. This pattern of perfection is not disturbed until chapter 3, when the first humans disobey God's command, and so disrupt the original order and introduce all kinds of disorder. Thistles and thorns, floods and earthquakes, disease, danger and death are *un*natural. The world inherited by the human race ever since is a second-hand remould. The rest of the Bible never questions this imagery and longs for a future when this original disorder is eliminated.

> Behold I create new heavens and a new
>   earth;
> and the former things shall not be
>   remembered...
> Behold I create Jerusalem a rejoicing...
> No more shall be heard in it the sound of
> weeping and the cry of distress...
> They shall not labour in vain,
> or bear children in calamity...
> The wolf and the lamb shall feed together,
> and the lion shall eat straw like the ox,
> and dust shall be the serpent's food.
> They shall not hurt or destroy
> in all my holy mountain, says the Lord.
>
> Isaiah 65: 17–25
>
> I saw a new heaven and a new earth...
> I heard a loud voice from the throne saying,
> 'Behold the dwelling of God is with men...
> He will wipe away every tear from their eyes,
> and death shall be no more,
> neither shall there be mourning
> nor crying nor pain any more,
> for the former things have passed away.'
>
> Revelation 21: 1–4

In fact the Genesis story is rather naïve. The author could not possibly have *asserted* that this was precisely how things began – he simply did not know. His primitive science and crude theodicy are simply the framework of a much more complicated message he has to preach.

The scientific truth is that natural disasters did not begin at some late moment of the universe's history, but are part and parcel of its make-up from the beginning. Disease and death dominated the dinosaur age, long before humans could commit their 'original sin'. The Genesis story of Adam and Eve has much to say about the human condition, but not about the origin of evil.

Of course, even when the unhistorical nature of the Genesis story is acknowledged, its suggestion that the world's evil is the fault of humans, not of God, continues to be stressed in what is known as the **Freewill**

Solution. According to this, human beings have always had the freedom to choose between good and evil. Much of the world's agony is the result of human hatred, greed, selfishness, envy and cruelty. If only people would choose to love, to care for each other and the environment, to be generous and to forgive, the world would no longer be the bedlam it so frequently turns into.

This is true. But sadly this freewill 'solution' does not begin to deal with the monstrous suffering caused, not only to humans but to the whole world of animals, by natural disasters, most of which have nothing to do with human freewill.

Evil is a punishment

God is quite justified in his relationship with evil. He has created it for the purpose of punishing those who do not do as he asks (or perhaps did not do so in a previous incarnation?). This is the most popular response to the problem of evil. Even pious people (indeed pious people in particular) presume that their sufferings (bereavement, accidents, sickness) are deliberately sent by God ('What have I done to deserve this?'). It is the solution most frequently appealed to in the Jewish Bible, especially in the Deuteronomic Collection (Deuteronomy, Joshua, Judges, Samuel, Kings) where every success is interpreted as a reward for virtue, and every setback as a punishment for sin. The solution continues to be used as a big stick right down to the last pages of the Christian New Testament.

> If you obey the voice of the Lord your God... all these blessings shall come upon you... Blessed shall you be in the city, and blessed shall you be in the field. Blessed shall be the fruit of your body, and the fruit of your ground, and the fruit of your beasts... The Lord will open to you his good treasury the heavens, to give the rain of your land in its season and to bless all the work of your hands.

But if you will not obey the voice of your God ... then all these curses shall come upon you and overtake you. Cursed shall you be in the city, and cursed shall you be in the field. Cursed shall be your basket and your kneading-trough ... The Lord will send upon you curses, confusion and frustration, in all that you undertake to do, until you are destroyed and perish quickly, on account of the evil of your doings ... The Lord will smite you with consumption, and with fever, inflammation, and fiery heat, and with drought, and with blasting, and with mildew; they shall pursue you until you perish. And the heavens over your head shall be brass, and the earth under you shall be iron.

Deuteronomy 28: 1–23

Come out of her (Rome) my people, lest you take part in her sins, lest you share in her plagues; for her sins are heaped high as heaven, and God has remembered her iniquities ... her plagues shall come in a single day, pestilence and mourning and famine, and she shall be burned with fire; for mighty is the Lord who judges her.

Revelation 18: 4–8

There are, of course, pages in the Bible which disagree with this solution, and most strongly in the psalms sung by suffering innocents, who protest vehemently that suffering must not be identified with sin. The whole Book of Job is similarly written to repudiate, nine times over, this traditional link between misfortune and guilt. Job suffers *in spite of* his innocence. And the Songs of the Suffering Servant (Isaiah 42–53) finally claim that suffering is a sign that one is a friend of God, not an enemy. The Books of Ecclesiastes and Jeremiah agree.

There is a vanity (absurdity) which takes place on earth, that there are righteous men to whom it happens according to the deeds of the wicked, and there are wicked men to whom it happens according to the deeds of the righteous. I said that this also is vanity.

Ecclesiastes 8: 14

Why does the way of the wicked prosper? Why do all who are treacherous thrive? Thou plantest them and they take root ... Thou art near in their mouth, but far from their heart.

Jeremiah 12: 1–2

The disagreement is strongest in the New Testament, where Jesus urges his followers to forgive those who offend them indiscriminately, because that is precisely what *God* does.

He makes his sun shine on good and bad alike,
his gentle rain falls on saints and on sinners ...
You must be perfect as your Father is,
he's kind to those who never thank him.

Matthew 5: 45–8
translated by H. J. Richards

His disciples asked him, 'Rabbi, who has sinned, this man or his parents, that he was born blind?'
Jesus answered, 'It was not that this man sinned, or his parents.'

John 9: 2–3

Indeed, for Christians, it would blasphemous to suppose that people in developing countries continue to starve because they have offended God, while people in the West prosper because they are in God's good books.

Evil is a test

God's association with evil is justified because he uses it to encourage growth. Evil is a deliberate challenge, which tests loyalty, stimulates discipline and builds character. Nothing of value can be achieved without risk and costliness. According to St Irenaeus (130–202 CE), our painful world is a 'Vale of Soul-Making', a kind of heavenly Duke of Edinburgh course.

This solution to the problem of evil is well represented in the Jewish and Christian traditions.

> *My son, do not despise the Lord's discipline*
> *or be weary of his reproof,*
> *for the Lord reproves him whom he loves,*
> *as a father the son in whom he delights.*
>
> Proverbs 3: 11–12
>
> *God tested Abraham:*
> *Take your son, your only son Isaac, whom*
> *you love*
> *and go the land of Moriah,*
> *and offer him there as a burnt offering'...*
> *'Do not lay your hand on the lad or do*
> *anything to him;*
> *for now I know that you fear God,*
> *seeing you have not withheld your son,*
> *your only son, from me.'*
>
> Genesis 22: 1–12
>
> *God is treating you as sons;*
> *for what son is there*
> *whom his father does not discipline?...*
> *He disciplines us for our own good*
> *that we may share his holiness.*
> *For the moment, all discipline seems painful,*
> *but later it yields*
> *the peaceful fruit of righteousness.*
>
> Hebrews 12: 7–11
>
> *For a little while you may have to suffer*
> *various trials, so that the genuineness of*
> *your faith, more precious than gold which*
> *though perishable is tested by fire, may*
> *redound to praise and glory and honour.*
>
> 1 Peter 1: 6–7

The Irenaean argument, as it has become known, has been developed and refined through the ages, never more strongly than by John Hick (b. 1922), who stresses the developmental nature of life, especially of human life. Humans are not born perfect: perfection comes at the end of the process, not the beginning. Virtue is not a given: it has to be achieved. This cannot be done freely without the disciplinary challenge of evil and suffering. Only through this challenge can the virtues of courage, compassion and self-sacrifice be formed. The alternative would be a world peopled by well-behaved puppets. The evil in the world will ultimately be justified by the infinite good that will come out of it.

There is obviously some truth in this solution. Many are indeed ennobled by suffering. But then again, many others are crippled. And would not an omniscient God already know his creatures without needing to put them to the test? Certainly a God who would construct an obstacle race to build up the muscles of some, while the rest fall by the wayside, is a monster – as the author of the Jewish Book of Job angrily points out.

> *What is man, that thou dost make so much*
> *of him,*
> *and that thou dost set thy mind upon him,*
> *dost visit him every morning,*
> *and test him every moment?*
> *How long wilt thou not look away from me,*
> *nor let me alone till I swallow my spittle?*
> *If I sin, what do I do to thee, thou*
> *Watcher of Men?*
> *Why hast thou made me thy mark?*
> *Why have I become a burden to thee?*
>
> Job 7: 17–10

> *Some think God tortures us because he*
> *loves us so much.*
> *What a shame he does not hate us, and*
> *treat us kindly.*
> *Thus: every evening, regularly, for six or*
> *seven years,*
> *The inoffensive and devout middle-aged*
> *woman,*
> *Lights a candle in front of a favoured*
> *religious image,*
> *And prays intently, I do not know what for,*
> *But it was not for this. One night, the candle*
> *Catches the hem of her highly flammable*
> *nightdress,*
> *Envelopes her in flames and burns her to*
> *death.*
> *Thus she is taken off to meet her God of Love,*
> *Possibly with a ready question on her lips.*

> *Let us hope he was wearing some means of identification.*
> *He could so easily be mistaken for his opposite number*
> *By anyone who judges character in the light of actions.*
>
> Frank Kuppner, *Last Eternal Moments*

Resignation

God's excuse for the existence of evil in his world is the same as that of a weaver of a piece of tapestry. He does not need to apologize for the chaos of knots, crossed threads and loose ends on the back of his work. The beauty of the end result on *the other side* could not be achieved without them. Evil is only the shadow of good, and it has to be accepted in the darkness of faith for the sake of the final glory.

> *I consider that the sufferings of the present time are not worth comparing with the glory that is to be revealed to us.*
>
> Romans 8:18
>
> *In paradise, God prepares for righteous believers what no eye has ever seen, nor ear has ever heard, and what the deepest mind could never imagine.*
>
> Saying of Muhammad 570–632 CE
>
> *Evil will always exist, always at odds with the good. It can find no place with God in heaven, only on earth. That is why we should try to escape from earth to heaven as quickly as we can.*
>
> Plato 429–347 BCE

There may again be elements of truth in this solution. Eggs have unfortunately to be broken to make an omelette, and it is obvious that good can quite often come out of evil. But it is also obvious that worse evil can come out of evil, indeed out of good itself. And if God is powerful enough to ensure a happy ending *on the other side*, why does he not exercise that power here and now on this side?

There is also a certain armchair callousness in the abstract acceptance of evil for the sake of a future good, which would sound totally irresponsible in the face of suffering itself – an endless line of refugees being machine-gunned, a drought killing off thousands of animals and humans, the liquidation of six million Jews in concentration camps.

Jesus' own reaction to the death of a friend was not to praise God's inscrutable plans, but to weep (John 11:36). In *The Brothers Karamazov* (1880) the Russian novelist Dostoyevsky shouts in anger against a philosophy which justifies the suffering of innocent children by the escapist promise of future bliss and glory. It would have been better, he maintains, if a universe which requires such suffering had never been created.

A package deal

Evil (in the shape of natural disasters) is neither 'sent' by God, nor 'allowed' by God (as if he could have decided otherwise). It is quite simply an inevitable part of the kind of world we live in, which is offered to us as a package deal, take it or leave it.

Ours is an evolutionary world, where human beings are the laborious end-product of the explosion of millions of stars. It is a world subject to fixed physical laws, where the slightest adjustment that one might wish to make would have produced a totally different world. It is a world where growth can only be achieved by overcoming opposition, and where original perfection is impossible: goodness can only be the fruit of trial and error. God is certainly to be held responsible for such a world, but so are the people whom he invites to be his co-creators.

> *A world similar to our own, the same but for the elimination of occasional catastrophes, is easy to imagine, but quite impossible. The strength of steel alloy, or its tendency to fatigue fracture, is determined, not arbitrarily as scientists might have thought*

only a hundred years ago, but according to sub-atomic forces which are in turn not arbitrary. Natural laws are now known to be part of a coherent interdependent pattern of order. The imaginable world in which steel had twice its strength would be completely different in every other respect, and man would not be around to enjoy its benefits...

A world in which disasters and famines occur, unchecked by divine intervention, is the only possible one God could have created with God in it.

Clifford Longley in *The Times*, 1985

The earth has cooled enough to form a crust, and on this crust life has emerged. If the earth had cooled more, to become solid and cold, there would be no life. Likewise of course if the earth was molten there would be no foothold even for vegetation. The earth has cooled enough to form a crust, whilst retaining enough warmth for life to emerge. These are the conditions which allow for earthquakes and volcanoes.

We might wish it were otherwise. But to exist is to exist with a life of one's own, whether it is as an atom, a cell, a multicellular structure, a shifting plate or an erupting volcano. To ask to exist without a life of one's own is to ask not to exist. Furthermore, this may or may not be the best of all possible worlds, but it is the only world we have got. So far as we can see, this kind of world, in which we are vulnerable and prone to accident, is the only world there could be for the emergence of beings with a genuine freedom of choice in relation to God and to one another.

Bishop Richard Harries in the *Independent*, 1988

For discussion

Are you happy with this acceptance of an imperfect world as the only possible world?

God can allow an earthquake

A CHRISTIAN SOLUTION? ■

PERHAPS none of the solutions listed above should be rejected outright. Each may have some element of a fuller answer. All the same, each of them (as we have seen) has considerable shortcomings and none of them is totally satisfying.

This could be because the God of classical theology stands behind all of them and he creates an impasse. A worthier solution of the problem might require a totally different understanding of God, as other sections of this book have already indicated (see pages 31 and 104). It could be that we must turn back from the God of the Philosophers to the God of the Bible, from the God of Aquinas's Three Ways (see page 15) and Newton's billiard table (see page 70) and Paley's watch (see page 18) – to the God of Abraham, Isaac, Jacob and Jesus.

The God of the Bible is an *incarnate* God, not remote and distant, but close at hand, present to his creatures and sharing in their condition. His unchangeability does not refer to a disinterested detachment, but to his steadfastness and dependability. His almighty power is not one of compulsion, but only of a self-giving love which overcomes all opposition. He is not absent from the evil in his universe, but present to draw good out of it, not as part of a plan, but simply because love conquers all. He is as vulnerable as his creatures are, and suffers with them. He is a God who is best understood before a crucifix.

This Christian response to evil is not proposed as a *theoretical* solution to the problem. There is none. As Job had already discovered, the problem will never be anything other than part of the cosmic mystery of God. But the story of Christ offers a *practical* approach to the problem and enables people to cope with the suffering and disaster that comes their way.

In the middle of one of his epistles (Romans 8: 18–39), St Paul paints a shrewd picture of the world as he sees it. It creaks and groans, it is frustrated and frustrating. It is a place of hardship and persecution, of calamity and ultimately death. And we are not to call these good, as if they are working together for our good: they're clearly not. But we are to call them less strong than the love of God. The calamities remain calamities, not hidden blessings. But through all of them, God continues to work for our good.

Christians see the supreme example of this in the death of Jesus. Not that they point to the cross and say, 'Isn't that beautiful!' It was not: it was the epitome of evil. But if God can be present, as love, even in the midst of that, is there anywhere he is absent?

This, of course, needs some believing. But it is a believing in *God*, not in things. It means trying to believe in a God who will not magically change things, who will let things be and not interfere to put them right, and whose presence therefore will often feel like an absence. It means trying to believe that in all things, in all circumstances, in all the events of our life, good and evil, we are loved; and that this love of God is stronger than all things put together.

Process theologians in particular (see page 30), having pointed to the chasm that lies between the God of classical philosophy (static, abstract, impassive) and the vulnerable God displayed in the life of Jesus, insist that a God who is in process (as all reality is) cannot do other than share the suffering of his creatures. A God of sheer power makes the problem of evil insoluble. A God as present in evil as he is in everything else, but in process of overcoming it, at least remains with us, not against us.

For discussion

Do the following reflections on evil make the problem less or even more perplexing?

What is there hid in the heart of a rose,
  mother mine?
Ah, who knows, who knows, who knows?
A man that died on a lonely hill
may tell you, perhaps, but none other will,
  little child.
What does it take to make a rose, mother
  mine?
The God that died to make it knows.
It takes the world's eternal wars,
it takes the moon and all the stars,
it takes the might of heaven and hell
and the everlasting love as well,
little child.

                    Alfred Noyes (1880–1958)

Omnipotent as I am,
'allowing' and 'preventing' is not within
  my power.
I have created a vulnerable world
where fire not only warms people but also
  burns them,
where water not only slakes their thirst
but also drowns them.
Who but plastic robots would live in a world
that was otherwise?
Given the world as it is, what's the use of a
  prayer

that two and two don't make four?
Or should I turn iron girders into rubber
if they fall on people's heads?
What people need to understand is
that in disasters I am not absent,
but more present than ever,
I am the God seen in Jesus,
more present (and heartbroken) in his
   tragic death
even than in his radiant life.
And more anxious than ever in 'bad times'
than in 'good times'
that people reveal my presence
in the love they show for each other.
'How can anyone find God in this situation?'
people say.
How can anyone help fish find the ocean?

H. J. Richards, *God's Diary*

Those who hear the message of the
resurrection of Christ, and no longer hear
the cry of the crucified contained in it, no
longer hear the Gospel, but a myth.

Johann Metz

Calvary was only a piece of it,
the piece that we saw, in time.
But the dark ring goes up and down
the whole length of the tree.
We only see it where it is cut across.
That is what Christ's life was:
the bit of God that we saw.
And because Christ was like that,
kind and forgiving sins and healing people,
we think God is like that.
And we think God is like that for ever
because it happened once to Christ.
But not the pain. Not the agony.
We think that stopped!
All the pain of the world was Christ's cross.
God's cross. And it goes on.

Helen Waddell (1889–1965),
Peter Abelard

Nowhere did it become more clearly visible
than in Jesus' life and work, suffering and
death, that this God is a God for men, a God
who is wholly on our side. He is not a
theocratical God, creating fear, 'from

above', but a God friendly to men, suffering
with men, 'with us below'.

Hans Küng, *On Being a Christian*

Through the clouds of Calvary – there shines
His face, and I believe that Evil dies,
And Good lives on, loves on, and conquers
   all –
All War must end in Peace. These clouds
   are lies.
They cannot last. The blue sky is the Truth.
For God is Love. Such is my Faith, and such
My reasons for it, and I find them strong
Enough. And you? You want to argue? Well,
I can't. It is a choice. I chose the Christ.

G. A. Studdert Kennedy,
Faith, The Unutterable Beauty

*One senses the genuine agony that lies
behind the discussion, say, of the innocent
suffering of a child, but to define the
problem in terms of how this can be
'meant', and therefore justified, in terms of
an Almighty Being who permits it, is to
distort the issue from the beginning...*

*God is in the cancer as he is in the sunset,
and is to be met and responded to in each.
Both are the faces of God, the one terrible,
the other beautiful. Neither as such is the
face of love, but, as in the Cross for the
Christian, even the worst can be
transformed and 'vanquished'. The
'problem' of evil is not how God can will it,
but its power to threaten and to sour...*

*The evil in the world is indeed terrifyingly
real, both at the subpersonal and the
personal level, but it is still part of the face
of God. That is to say, love is there to be
met and to be created through it and out of
it. It is not without purpose: meaning can be
wrested from it even at the cost of
crucifixion. It is not separate from the face
of love, and therefore cannot separate from
it. That is the saving grace: God is not
outside evil any more than he is outside
anything else, and the promise is that he
'will be all in all' as love.*

J. A. T. Robinson, *Exploration into God*

While God cannot be said to be responsible for the world's evil, he has assumed responsibility for it by creating a world such as ours in the first place. That is to say, he is not a distant God, but somehow present even in the evil, loving and caring for those who suffer it, and enabling people to triumph over it by bringing good out of evil.

We are able to say this as Christians because we believe that God was present in the crucifixion of Jesus Christ, where evil was fundamentally conquered. The worst that humans can do cannot make God swerve from his mercy towards us, but becomes the means of final victory. It would of course be misleading to say that God suffers when we suffer. But it would be equally misleading to say that God does not suffer. The Christian faith is that the best clue we have to the nature of God is Jesus suffering and dying for us on the cross.

Peter de Rosa, *Private Notes*

SAMPLE EXAM QUESTIONS

1 For what reasons may suffering create philosophical problems for a religious believer? Outline two solutions to these problems and comment on their success.

(Edexcel AS sample paper)

2 Explain how the theodicy of Irenaeus differs from that of Augustine.

(OCR AS sample paper)

3 'Natural evil is not explained by the need for free will.' Discuss.

(OCR AS sample paper)

4 How successful are Christian answers to the challenge of natural disasters?

(OCR AS and A sample paper)

5 'We should explain ourselves to God; he does not have to explain himself to us.' How adequate is this as a response to the problem of evil?

(OCR A sample paper)

6 'God is the omnipotent and wholly good creator of all things.' 'There is evil in the world.' Explain these two statements, and show why they are said to be contradictory. To what extent does Hick's soulmaking theodicy remove the contradiction?

(AQA A sample paper)

6 *God and science*

The relationship between religion and science is an uneasy one. They have frequently been in tension with each other and at times in open conflict. Such a strained relationship is not inevitable, as we shall see – there have always been scientists who have found their religion a help in their task, not a hindrance, and never more so than in today's world.

Nevertheless the scientist and the believer look at the world from quite different standpoints, so that what one says often clashes with what is being said by the other. As an extreme example of such a clash, consider the statement made by Bertrand Russell (1872–1970):

I regard religion as a disease born of fear, and as a source of untold misery to the human race.

Why would such an eminent friend of science say something so violent?

THE CASE AGAINST RELIGION

Religion is irrational

Science deals with the real world of hard facts – visible, tangible, demonstrable, provable and verifiable. In contrast, the world to which religion keeps referring seems to be unreal, made up of things which are quite unverifiable, in fact not even visible (angels, devils, heaven, hell, God, salvation, soul, etc.). No convincing proof is offered of the reality of these things, so that the very discussion of them seems to many people to be totally irrational.

> *The cosmos is a gigantic flywheel making 10,000 revolutions a minute. Man is a sick fly taking a dizzy ride on it. Religion is the theory that the wheel was designed and set spinning to give man the ride.*
>
> H. L. Mencken (1880–1956)

Religion is escapist

The appeal that religion makes to 'another' world suggests a reluctance to face the harsh reality of this world, and an infantile escape into fantasy. Hence the invention of a powerful Father-figure as a protector against the ills and bogeymen with which this world is beset. Hence too the reliance on primitive beliefs and practices which a world-come-of-age recognizes as sheer childish superstition. As the world grows more and more mature, it becomes less and less religious.

Excerpts from a popular prayer book published with ecclesiastical approval in Mainz, Germany, in 1647.

A safeguard against plague

Reputed to come from St Zacharias, bishop of Jerusalem, via the Patriarch of Antioch, who was concerned when twenty bishops attending the Council of Trent in 1547 died of the plague, and advised all the other bishops to carry the following letters on their person, and to inscribe them over the doors of those needing protection:

+ Z + DJA + BJZ + SAB + ZHGF + BFRS.

The St Benedict penny

To be blessed by the priest, and carried devoutly on the person. It guarantees:

- Protection from all witchcraft and devilry.
- Prevention of any witch or wizard entering a house where the coin is nailed to the door or buried under the threshold.
- Release of any animal that has been possessed or bewitched (wash the animal with water in which the coin has been laid).
- When a cow gives bad milk, put the coin in water and make the cow drink it.

Against worms

Say three times:

Peter and Jesus went into the field,
They ploughed three acres and ploughed up
*   three worms,*
One was white, one was black, one was red,
And so all the worms were dead.
In the name of + the Father and of + the Son
*   and of + the Holy Ghost.*

To stop bleeding

Breathe on the patient three times, and then say the Our Father *three times as far as 'be done on earth', and the bleeding will stop.*

To win at dice

Use a red silk ribbon to bind the heart of a bat on the throwing arm. Guaranteed.

For safety in all circumstances

Write out the following blessing and carry it on you:

Christ walked in peace among his disciples,
St Matthew, St Mark, St Luke, St John.
May these four Evangelists,
through the sublime Majesty and one
*   Godhead JJJ Amen*
J. G. B. J. J. R. 8121
stay with me for ever + + + Amen.

For discussion

It is improbable that any of these strange superstitious practices still exist. But many others, just as strange, continue to take their place. Why do you think this is so?

Religion is obscurantist

Religion has not only promoted immaturity, but positively hampered growth and progress by its authoritarianism, dogmatism, coercion and intolerance.

Where the rule by ecclesiastics (hierarchy) replaces rule by consent (democracy), where research is suspect and books are censored, where the unorthodox are spied upon (inquisition) and tortured, where free speech is denied and witches are burnt, and all in the name of God – then it is time to abandon God and realize that religion is nothing other than the National Front dressed in holy vestments.

It has become what Marx called it: an 'opium' that deadens people's sensitivity and makes them incapable of dealing with life in the real world.

This new invention (printing)... has allowed people to call into question the Church's faith and doctrines. Lay people are reading the Bible, and praying in their own language... The mysteries of religion must be kept in the hands of the priests.

Cardinal Wolsey
in a letter to Pope Clement VII, 1525

Lightning, it is well known, can damage and even destroy the tree or building that it strikes. When Benjamin Franklin invented the 'lightning conductor' in 1752 (to deflect the flash safely along a low-resistance cable into the earth) many churchmen condemned it as a 'heretic-rod', interfering with what was obviously a heaven-sent punishment of God.

To claim that everyone should be granted and guaranteed freedom of conscience is one of the most contagious of errors, false and absurd, in fact insane.

Pope Gregory XVI, 1832

Freedom of worship is a liberty totally contrary to the virtue of religion.

Pope Leo XIII, 1885

Anyone who has never been angry against religion has not known too much about it.

Anon.

Crusaders versus Muslims

A reporter visiting the Roman Catholic shrine in Medjugorje in the former Yugoslavia wrote home about the monument erected to the Croat who cut the throats of 1400 Serbian men, women and children; and about the UN convoy, taking food and medicine to the battered Mostar Muslims, which was blockaded by the women of Medjugorje sitting on the road singing hymns.

Religion is divisive

Even though all forms of religion preach reconciliation and peace, they have throughout history produced friction, division and the most cruel of wars.

Witness:

- Israelites versus Canaanites under Joshua
- Crusaders versus Muslims under successive popes
- Christian persecution of Jews from the Middle Ages down to modern times (Hitler presumed Christians would approve)
- Protestants martyred by Catholics under Queen Mary, and vice versa under Queen Elizabeth
- Islam versus Judaism
- Hindus versus Sikhs
- Orthodox Serbs versus Muslims in Kosovo, Muslims versus Christians in East Timor and Nigeria
- The apparently unbridgeable Protestant–Catholic divide in Northern Ireland.

Since religion insists that these wars are waged in the name of God, any appeal to a higher authority remains impossible.

Anyone who wants to know all about Christianity should read the Sermon on the Mount. Anyone who wants to know even more about Christianity should read the history of its relationship with Judaism.

Rabbi J. Magonet, 1970

In contrast

All the progress made by the human race in its long history has come about independently of religion, and often despite it. Where religion has tended to ascribe all the dark areas to God, science has gone on and on pushing back the barriers, searching, recording, measuring, counting, listing, experimenting and modifying.

This painstaking method has built up a body of knowledge which stands on its own feet without any reference to God, which has taken charge of our world and changed it for the better, and which works for believers and non-believers alike. Insisting as it does, on testing everything, and on taking nothing on anyone's say so (*Nullius in verbo* – the motto of the Royal Society), its sheer commitment to truth *at all costs* can only be admired.

Fundamentally, religion is afraid of life. It is a running away from life. It disparages life here and now as merely the preliminary to a fuller life beyond. Mysticism and religion mean that life here on earth is a failure; that independent man is not good enough to achieve salvation. But free children do not feel that life is a failure, for no one has taught them to say nay to life.

A. S. Neill, *Summerhill*

(Religion) demands that no other kind of perspective shall be accorded any value, after one has rendered one's own

sacrosanct with the names 'God', 'redemption', 'eternity'... Wherever the influence of the theologian extends, value judgement is stood on its head, the concepts 'true' and 'false' are necessarily reversed, that which is most harmful to life is here called 'true', and that which enhances, intensifies, affirms, justifies it and causes it to triumph is called 'false'... Wherever there are walls I shall inscribe this eternal accusation against Christianity upon them...I call Christianity the one great curse, the one great intrinsic depravity, the one great instinct for revenge for which no expedient is sufficiently poisonous, secret, subterranean, petty – I call it the one immortal blemish of mankind.

Friedrich Nietzsche,
The Anti-Christ

I will respect your views if you can justify them. But if you justify your views only by saying you have faith in them, I shall not respect them...Science offers us an explanation of how complexity (the difficult) arose out of simplicity (the easy). The hypothesis of God offers no worthwhile explanation for anything, for it simply postulates what we are trying to explain. It postulates the difficult to explain, and leaves it at that. We cannot prove that there is no God, but we can safely conclude that He is very, very improbable indeed..

Dr Richard Dawkins, International
Science Festival, Edinburgh, 1992

For discussion

Once again, do you see these angry objections as overstatements or understatements?

THE CASE FOR RELIGION ■

Religion has the majority

The western world so dominates events that it is often thought of as the only world there is. And since it has in the recent past increasingly turned its back on religion ('secularization') and is referred to as the 'developed' world, it is often assumed that secularization is now universal, or will be as soon as the developing ('third') world catches up.

In actual fact, even today the number of people in the world for whom religion is vitally important continues to be far greater than that of non-believers.

Out of a world population of about
6000 million, there are about:

2000 m	Christians
1200 m	Islam
900 m	Hinduism
350 m	Buddhism
225 m	Confucianism
190 m	Primal religions
20 m	Yoruba religion
18 m	Sikhism
15 m	Judaism
7 m	Shinto
6 m	Bahai
4 m	Jainism
3 m	Tao
36 m	Others

4974 m = about 83% of world population

Internet (adherents.com) March 2000

If these numbers are taken back across the whole of human history, the percentage of non-believers is so small as hardly to count.

This is not a knock-down argument – all believers could be wrong! But the burden of proof would be enormous.

Culture is rooted in religion

Every human culture, in the past as in the present, in the east as in the west, has been shaped by religion. Ancient Assyria, Babylonia, Persia, Greece and Rome no longer rule the civilized world, but their magnificent monuments still bear witness to the central role played by religion in the life of each. And anyone visiting Cairo or Shanghai or Tehran today will see how the very skyline of mosques, minarets and temples still bears witness to the importance of religion.

Turning to the Christian west, very little research is needed to reveal how deeply the whole of Europe is the product of its Christian past. Europe became known as 'Christendom' not only because Christians built a lot of cathedrals and churches – which even today still attract more visitors than many other tourist sites – but because it was the Christian faith that for centuries inspired the whole of its culture: its architecture, its literature, its painting, its sculpture, its music, its laws, its calendar – even its customs and folklore. Easterners are even able to recognize western atheism as a 'Christian' atheism!

As before, this is not a proof that the religious heritage of both east and west is 'right'. But it suggests that this heritage may not be dismissed as if it is a nothing.

Religion asks the deep questions

There is no denying that science has been highly successful in the scope it has set itself. But this is because the scope is deliberately limited to the manageable questions: 'what?', 'when?', 'where?', 'who?', 'how?'. And in measuring, counting, tabulating, weighing, comparing and analysing the answers to these two-dimensional questions, science has been brilliant.

But truth has more than two dimensions, especially the truth about human beings. Religion is concerned about this third dimension, which asks the deeper question: 'why?', and looks for the purpose of our world, its values, and its meanings.

Science speaks of humanity as Shakespeare's Macbeth does, as an absurd and meaningless story – the end result of blind and random forces. Is this account closer to the truth and more worthwhile than the one given by the Psalmist and Shakespeare's Hamlet (see the boxes below)? How important is it to describe the world, not only in terms of length and breadth and weight and size, but also (as theologians do) in terms of love, courage, self-sacrifice, caring, forgiveness, compassion, prudence, fortitude, hope, self-control, honour, duty, service, trust, fidelity, respect, discretion, diligence, conscientiousness, responsibility, perseverance, etc.? Scientists make scant reference to these qualities. Does that make them less important?

Life is but a walking shadow, a poor player
That struts and frets his hour upon the stage,
And then is heard no more: it is a tale
Told by an idiot, full of sound and fury,
Signifying nothing.

Macbeth V, 5, 17

What a piece of work is man! How noble in reason! How infinite in faculty! In form, in moving, how express and admirable! In action how like an angel! In apprehension how like a god! The beauty of the world! The paragon of animals!

Hamlet II, 2, 316

When I see the heavens, the work of your
  hands,
the moon and the stars which you arranged,
what are we that you should keep us in mind,
mere mortals that you care for us?
Yet you have made us little less than gods,
and crowned us with glory and honour,
you gave us power over the work of your hands,
put all things under our feet.
All of them, sheep and cattle,
yes, even the savage beasts,
birds of the air, and fish
that make their way through the waters.
How great is your name, o Lord our God,
through all the earth.

Psalm 8, Grail Version

O Lord, illumine my heart with light,
my sight with light and my hearing with light.

*Let there be light on my right hand and on
my left,
light behind me and light going before me …
O God, who knows the innermost secret of
our hearts,
lead us out of the darkness into the light.*

Prayer of Muhammad

*People say Christianity is just common
sense. It is nothing of the kind. It is very
uncommon non-sense. What on earth –
that is, in material terms – makes less
sense than to suppose that an all-wise,
all-powerful and benevolent Spirit should
want to create mankind? … Man with his
wars and cruelties, his thumbscrews and
his prisons, his tortures and rapes and
mutilations … We go on to believe, not
only that a loving God created man, but
that he loved him … even after Hiroshima
and all that has happened since. What
could be more unreasonable than to
believe that? …*

*Yet, out of this welter of cruelty and
bloodshed that is the history of man, there
has somehow grown pity for others and self-
sacrificing love, shared meals, shared lives,
shared laughter, sweet singing in the choir
… So let us not try to make Christianity
reasonable.*

Philip Mason, *The Tablet*, 1991

*The fallacy of a positivist approach to
science is that if you search the universe for
certain kinds of connections, these are* the
only ones *you will find. Everything else
slips through the net. God does not appear
in the scientific account of nature because
the objectives and methods are impervious
to anything that might point to God: any hint
of purpose or intention or feeling or value…*

*Religious experience points to truths that
elude this kind of treatment – our
knowledge of people, for instance, or
historical knowledge, or the kind of truth
that can only be conveyed in stories.*

Archbishop T. Hapgood,
the *Independent*, 1992

*We are told that religion has ceased to
matter. What an insular view! Religion at all
times and in all places reaches into the
deepest depths of the human psyche, and in
most parts of the world is still, perhaps, the
major determinant of the social order. In
Latin America, in Asia south and southeast,
in Iran, in large parts of Africa, in eastern
Europe, in the Middle East, and on our own
doorstep in Northern Ireland, religion has in
recent years been a major agent of social
change, with profound political and
economic effects, and has shown an
inexhaustible capacity to inspire people at
all levels of society to re-examine critically
the meaning and conditions of their
existence.*

*Whether or not we always approve of the
results is beside the point. The point is that
whether its force be regarded as malignant
or beneficial, religion is for large sections of
mankind a more powerful motivator than
the dollar exchange rate, or the lure of
material prosperity. That is some force by
any reckoning, and we minimize or scorn it
at our peril.*

J. F. X. Harriott, *The Tablet*, 1983

*We are sold short by mechanistic
explanations of the universe. The more
'facts' we know, the more the whole seems
greater than the parts. The more causes and
effects are identified, the more the most
vivid experience of being human seems left
out of account. And the more the
microscope and telescope reveal of the
simple laws which underpin all life, the
more the central mystery of the why and
wherefore clamours for an answer.*

*The cold rational universe we have been
offered during the age of science, its minutest
details docketed and documented, and its
reduction of man to one outgrowth among
many of chemistry, physics and biology, seems
to exclude all that is more intense, thrilling,
moving and perplexing in human experience.
Our dreams, our ideals, our conscience, our
inspirations, our responsibilities.*

What light does this multitude of facts shed upon love, courage or self-sacrifice? What light does it shed, for example, upon the action of a British soldier who threw himself at Arnhem on a hand-grenade to save the life of a Dutch mother and child? Or upon the passions and denial of passions that are the stuff of mankind's literature? Or the sense of moral obligation to a Supreme Being on which Newman set such store? Or on Auschwitz or the Gulag?...

The essential nature of our universe is not material but spiritual. The closer we get to the heart of reality the more we encounter the paradoxical and the inexplicable. The truest vision of the universe leads out of science, and indeed beyond rational thought and language.

J. F. X. Harriott, *The Tablet*, 1984

For discussion

Do you agree that there are human truths, ideals and values about which science has nothing to say? Give examples.

Religion is the Mother of Science

Far from hindering science, the Judaeo-Christian religion has (at least in principle) given birth to science through its doctrine of 'incarnation'. In such a faith, God is not in another world, or hived off in a sacred 'no-go' area of our world. On the contrary he is *in carne*, in the flesh and blood of secular history and human activity. It is this secular reality that has to be examined and explored if God is to be discovered.

This is not to claim that Christians have always followed the logic of their incarnational faith. They have often in practice denied it. But, *in principle*, the true believer wants more and more science, not less and less.

It should come as no surprise, therefore, to find that many of the greatest scientists in the West have been believers and have seen their work as an expression of their religious beliefs. Examples include Galileo, Descartes, Pascal, Newton, Pasteur, Einstein, Teilhard de Chardin, etc. In this context mention should also be made of the great reformers and pioneers in education, human rights, welfare, social services, etc. – the Nightingales, Frys, Wilberforces, Barnardos – for whom religion was not an obstacle in their work, but its inspiration.

If religion is based on faith, so is science

Finally, it is important to point out that if religion cannot claim to have a monopoly of truth, neither can science. It is one thing to have a rule that: 'What is proved should be accepted', but quite another to have a rule that: '*Only* what is proved should be accepted'. Such a rule cannot itself be proved!

Science does well to establish the facts. But those facts may be interpreted in different ways and lead to different conclusions. No one may be totalitarian and claim: 'Only *my* interpretation of the universe (this has meaning / this has no meaning) is valid'. The conclusion that science arrives at is just as much a faith as the conclusion arrived at by religion.

Finally, it ought not to be overlooked that if some religious people have been extreme and even savage, some irreligious people have too.

GREAT NAMES IN SCIENCE ▪

THE tension between religion and science is a fairly recent phenomenon. It is only with the rise of modern science that all kinds of unexamined assumptions (in physics, chemistry, botany, biology, anthropology, astronomy, geology, history, etc.) were unexpectedly challenged for the first time. This challenge did not necessarily involve conflict with religious beliefs, but it

Galileo

Protestantism then sweeping Europe, he was burnt in Rome in 1600.

All this pioneer work was finally brought together and widely publicized by the Italian mathematician and astronomer Galileo Galilei (born in the same year as Shakespeare). With the newly invented telescope, which he had boosted to a thousandfold magnification, he was able to confirm definitively the Copernican understanding of Planet Earth and its relationship to the heavens beyond.

Some sayings of Galileo

The Bible teaches us how to go to heaven, not how the heavens go.

Nature is as divine a text as the holy Scriptures. They can't be in real contradiction with each other.

Eppur si muove = *It (the earth) jolly well* does *move.*

certainly required the re-thinking and readjustment of much traditional teaching.

The following great thinkers, therefore, need to be considered not only negatively for their critique of certain traditional religious beliefs, but also positively for the contribution they made to a deeper understanding of ourselves and our planet.

Galileo Galilei 1564–1642

Until the middle of the 16th century, no one questioned the 'geocentric' astronomy of Ptolemy (150 CE), according to which the earth (*geo*) is static at the centre with the sun and planets revolving around it.

The first questions were raised in 1543 by the Polish monk Copernic(us), whose observations indicated that our planetary system is actually 'heliocentric' – centred on the sun (*helios*). In 1590, the German mathematician Kepler confirmed this 'Copernican Revolution', and in 1593 the Italian monk Giordano Bruno concluded that the geocentric story of creation in the Bible needed (at least) some reinterpretation. Out of fear that such ideas could encourage the

In 1633, aged 69, his conclusions were condemned by the Catholic Church as contradicting the Bible, and as absurd in any case ('If the earth moved around the sun, all Italian churches would fall down'). To avoid the death sentence, he agreed not to publicize his views any further, and had to accept the banning of all his books. He was put under house arrest for the last ten years of his life.

Over the last 350 years, astronomy has made even further advances and shown us that even the sun is far from central – it is only a small star in one of the 500 million galaxies. In the light of this, the Catholic Church's ban on Copernicus's writings was finally lifted in 1757, the Genesis account of creation was finally acknowledged to be unscientific in 1822, and a public apology was finally offered to Galileo in 1992. Even so, the word Galileo continues to carry overtones of a frightened and obscurantist religion trying desperately to suppress facts, and therefore continually at loggerheads with science.

Galileo has been called the 'Father of Modern Science', not only because of the *fact* that he challenged a whole number of suppositions never previously questioned (including the position of the human race in the universe), but because of the *method* he used. Truth, he maintained, was not to be discovered simply by asking the authorities (scripture, tradition, creeds) but by observation, experimentation and free enquiry. Such a method could eventually call everything into question.

For discussion

Do you feel that all people, or at least most people, could cope with this invitation to call everything into question?

René Descartes 1596–1650

This French mathematician and philosopher, a contemporary of Galileo, came to very similar conclusions about the *method* of arriving at truth and certainty. In his *Discourse on the Method of Right Reason* (1637) he called this method 'Universal Doubt'.

Supposing all those to whom I have normally gone to find out the truth are mistaken? What would happen if I systematically doubted every supposed source of certainty: divine revelation, tradition, dogma, the 'authorities', even the evidence of my own senses? Would anything be left on which I could build with confidence?

Only my own doubt – and myself as the doubter. 'I think, therefore (at least) *I am*.' That is certain. That cannot be doubted. At last a clear and unambiguous bottom line, a foundation on which to build the rest of my knowledge.

I resolved to pretend that nothing which had ever entered my mind was any more true than the illusions of my dreams. But immediately afterwards I became aware

that, while I decided thus to think that everything was false, it followed necessarily that I who thought thus must be something; and observing that this truth, 'I think therefore I am', was so certain and so evident that all the most extravagant suppositions of the sceptics were not capable of shaking it, I judged that I could accept it without scruple as the first principle of the philosophy I was seeking.

Descartes,
Discourse on the Method of Right Reason

From this basis, Descartes went on to establish the existence of God ('I can no more deny his existence than deny that a triangle has three sides'), the existence of the world outside of himself ('A perfect God would not deceive me'), and the clear distinction between soul–mind and body–matter ('I can think of myself without my body').

Descartes' daring to call everything into question, his bold claim of autonomy ('I am ruled from within, not from outside myself') and his insistence that everything must be judged by the light of the unaided human reason – all this entitles him to share with Galileo the title 'Father of Modern Science', and to be called the first modern critical thinker. He could not foresee that his views would lead others (as they had not led him) to humanism, secularism and atheism.

Note – Because the name Descartes translates into Latin as Cartesius, his philosophy is often referred to as 'Cartesian'.

For discussion

Are there things which ought not to be judged by reason alone?

Isaac Newton 1642–1727

Born in the year Galileo died, this brilliant British mathematician made deep explorations into the nature of light, established the law of gravity, formulated the binomial theorem, and contributed decisively to the development of infinitesimal calculus. Knighted in 1705, he was buried in Westminster Abbey.

Newton's most important contribution to science was to formulate the Laws of Motion. According to these, all bodies in motion will continue to move in a straight line unless acted upon by an opposing force. Thus, the total amount of energy expended in the universe, however widely distributed, will always be constant, like a machine in perpetual motion, or a billiard table hermetically sealed off from outside intervention (where the total force expended by a moving billiard ball would exactly equal the force originally applied by the player).

These simple, mechanical and unchanging laws explain all the physical facts of the universe and even allow us to predict the future. In the late 17th century they provided such a satisfying world-view that they remained unquestioned for the next 300 years, and Newton's *Principia Mathematica* was as highly respected as the Bible.

Nature, and Nature's laws lay hid in night;
God said, 'Let Newton be', and all was light.

Alexander Pope,
a contemporary of Newton's

If I have seen further, it is by standing on the shoulders of giants.

Isaac Newton

Newton had no desire to challenge the religion of his day. Indeed he saw his work as contributing to the greater glory of God. But it was a deistic God, who was little more than a Cosmic Clockmaker. Newton had put the finishing touches to Galileo's mechanical understanding of the universe, and to the rationalistic approach of Descartes. His 'deterministic' view of the world had little in common with the view offered by the Bible. Religion and science were by now very far apart.

For discussion

There is much that is deeply satisfying about Newton's billiard-table universe. Point out anything that is dissatisfying about it.

Charles Darwin 1809–82

Traditional '**Creationism**' or 'Fixism' holds that each species of living being was fixed from its creation onward. This was first challenged during the 19th century. Naturalists like Lamarck proposed an alternative theory of '**Transformism**', according to which organisms were gradually transformed by the environment in which they grew up, and passed these changed characteristics on to the next generation.

In 1831, Charles Darwin, aged only 22 and just graduated in theology from Cambridge, was invited to sail with the HMS *Beagle*, then making a survey of the South American coast, as the official government naturalist. Among his discoveries on the Galapagos Islands, 600 miles west of Ecuador, was the fact that the giant tortoises on different islands, though clearly related, were quite different from each other. He also noted that different finches had beaks of a different shape according to the food (seeds or insects or termites) they lived on. He concluded that it would be unreasonable to hold that God had once and for all *created* all these animals slightly different from each other, when it was more likely that they had all *evolved* differently from common ancestors.

Each change need be only minimal. But across many thousands of years these accumulated changes could explain vast differences between all living species. And there was no reason why they could not all have a common ancestry. This would include even humans.

As to how and why such an evolution should come about, he proposed a theory of **Natural Selection**, or survival of the fittest. In the struggle for survival, presumably those best adapted to their surroundings (by size, strength, speed, etc.) would live while others died. Indeed the planet could not possibly support all the creatures it produces. Within only 750 years, even a pair of slow breeding elephants could produce 19 million descendants!

> In a public debate at the British Association on 30 June 1860, Samuel Wilberforce, Bishop of Oxford, declared that if Darwin's theory of evolution was true, then Genesis was a lie, divine revelation a delusion, and God dethroned. He concluded by asking whether Darwin claimed to be descended from an ape through his grandfather or his grandmother.
>
> In reply the biologist Thomas Huxley, known as 'Darwin's Bulldog', said he would be less ashamed to have a monkey as his ancestor than a prejudiced intellectual who knew nothing about science and who used his great gifts to obscure the truth.

In 1859, Darwin published these findings in *The Origin of Species*. The edition sold out on the day of publication. He himself admitted that it was 'like confessing to a murder'. Racked by anxiety over the implications of his theory, he spent the last 40 years of his life a very sick man. He died aged 73 and was buried with great ceremony in Westminster Abbey.

Subsequent research into evolution (like Gregor Mendel's discovery in the 19th century of the existence of particles or 'genes' which transmit characteristics from one generation to another; and the further refinement of Mendel's work by the 1962 Nobel prize winners Francis Crick and his American colleague James Watson analysing the structure of the acid DNA which determines the genetic code) has modified some of Darwin's ideas, but never called his basic theory into question. Indeed the study of rock strata and the fossils found in them has strongly corroborated Darwin's findings, only extending Darwin's estimate of the earth's timespan from 300 million years to 4½ billion!

Neo-Darwinism (as it is called) has recently acquired a doughty champion in Richard Dawkins, whose defence and development of Darwin have conferred a new respectability on his revolutionary vision.

The picture of the universe emerging from Darwin's researches differs so strongly from what had previously been assumed by believers that religion and science seemed more incompatible than ever. God had been infinitely distanced. A designed universe had given way to random and blind chance. Humans were no longer God's darlings, but simply naked apes, alone in a universe without meaning.

> Napoleon   *'And what place does God have in your explanation of the universe?'*
> The naturalist Laplace   *'Sire, I have no need of such a hypothesis.'*   1804

Darwin himself found his hold on God growing weaker and weaker. Many one-time believers now abandoned religion as an outdated superstition. Others survived by living two different lives on weekdays and Sundays. Others remained believers by simply burying their head in the sand: witness the 1909 decree of the Biblical Commission in Rome that the opening chapters of the Book of Genesis must continue to be taken literally. The decree was not withdrawn until 1943.

> ### For discussion
> If humans are simply the end products of blind, random and selfish natural processes, how can there be any sort of obligation to lead a moral life?

Karl Marx 1818–83

The evolution which Darwin had discovered to be present in nature was discovered to be present in society and history as well by Karl Marx, a German Jew descended from a long line of rabbis. Editor of a left-wing newspaper, his radical political views forced him to flee, first to Paris and finally to London. Working with Friedrich Engels, he produced in 1848 the *Communist Manifesto*, outlining the ideal society which could be brought about if the working-class poor ('proletariat') rose up against their exploitative employers. His political philosophy was worked out in greater detail in *Das Kapital*, written in the British Museum between 1867 and 1871.

> *The time will come when the language of religion will be as useless as toy money.*
>
> Karl Marx
>
> *The workers have nothing to lose but their chains. They have a world to gain. Workers of the world, unite!*
>
> *Communist Manifesto*, 1848
>
> *The philosophers have hitherto only interpreted the world in various ways. The point is, however, to change it.*
>
> Inscription on Marx's grave in Highgate Cemetery

Marxist philosophy is fundamentally materialist. What is basic in our universe is not mind, spirit, thought or ideas – but matter. Not that matter is inert: it has an inbuilt principle of evolution which allows it eventually to become aware of itself, to develop a mind.

This evolution takes places in a process that Hegel called '**dialectic**'. A *thesis* is always being challenged by its opposite *antithesis*. Growth can only take place when the tension and struggle between them produces a *synthesis* which transcends both of them because it fuses the best of both.

History has always followed the same pattern. One political structure has evolved into another because that was the only way in which the inherent contradictions could be solved.

In *feudal society* serfs were in tension with their baron overlords. The Industrial Revolution changed this system into a *capitalist society* where factory owners denied the proletarian workers the fruits of their labour. These workers must now be 'conscientized' – made aware of the injustice of this situation, so that they seize power and form a *socialist society*. This will reach its perfection in a classless *communism* – an earthly paradise in which there will be no more selfish competition, because each will give according to his ability, and each receive according to his need.

Throughout history, Marx claimed, religion has hindered this (r)evolution by supporting the *status quo*. In this way it has become an opium, drugging and paralysing its adherents. It is only by throwing off its evil influence that people will become fully human.

There is a messianic (even biblical) quality in this respect of human dignity and this attack on rotten religion. Is it too idealist?

For discussion

Why do you think that no Marxist country (nor any religious country either!) has yet been able to achieve the Utopia Marx dreamed of?

20th century sociology

The pioneer founders of Sociology, Emile Durkheim (1858–1917) and Max Weber (1864–1920) agreed with Marx's analysis of society, but were less disparaging of religion. Durkheim judged religion not by its truth, but by its function as the 'glue' of society, giving it the cohesion without which society would disintegrate. Religion has provided this service throughout the centuries. Common beliefs and practices continue to provide a stability which makes religion not only valuable, but valid. Weber saw religion as an important catalyst producing the changes that society needs in order to prosper.

The philosopher and psychologist William James (1842–1910) was similarly positive about religion. To his way of thinking, truth can never be absolute, but only relative.

What is true is what works, if only for the time being. This does not invalidate religion. On the contrary, like love, religion adds to life an enchantment which nothing else can provide. People believe in God, not because they can prove he exists, but because they need a God. The varieties of religious experience consistently point to the existence of a whole reservoir of energies from which we are constantly refreshed. This is why people with religion cope with life far better than those without. 'Not God', he said, 'but life, more life, a larger, richer, more satisfying life, is in the last analysis the purpose of religion.' (*Varieties of Religious Experience*, 1902.)

The complex human personality, according to Freud, with the conscious *ego* sandwiched between the unconscious *superego* above and *id* below.

For discussion

In pointing to what really enhances life, are sociologists and psychologists revealing the reality of God, or watering it down?

Sigmund Freud 1865–1939

With Freud, the evolution which Darwin had discovered in nature, and Marx in society, enters inside people themselves. The mind also evolves.

Freud, a Viennese psychiatrist, pioneered the treatment of disturbed people by analysing their **psyche** or unconscious self, through dreams, role models, slips of the tongue, free association, etc. He revealed to his patients that their **ego** (self) is a battleground between the **superego** (conscience, whether well-formed or not) and the **id** (primitive and instinctual urges). Each person is a compromise between what he or she would like to do and what they feel they are allowed to do. Freud further succeeded in helping his patients recall the past repression of wishes and needs (often of a sexual kind) and to realize that when these realities are made conscious and analysed, healing may take place.

Humanity has, in the course of time, had to endure from the hands of science two great outrages upon its naïve self-love.

The first was when it realized that our earth was not the centre of the universe, but only a tiny speck in a world-system of a magnitude hardly conceivable (Galileo)...

The second was when biological research robbed man of his peculiar privilege of having been specially created, and relegated him to a descent from the animal world, implying an ineradicable animal nature in him (Darwin)...

But man's craving for grandiosity is now suffering the third and most bitter blow from present-day psychological research which is endeavouring to prove to the 'ego' of each one of us that he is not even master in his own house... We psychoanalysts were neither the first nor the only ones to propose to mankind that they should look inward; but it appears to be our lot to advocate it most insistently, and to support it by empirical evidence which touches every man closely.

Sigmund Freud,
Introductory Lectures on Psycho-Analysis

About 1900 years before Freud, St Paul had analysed the human self in the following terms.

I do not understand my own actions.
For I do not do what I want,
but I do the very thing I hate.
Now if I do what I do not want...
it is no longer I that do it,
but sin which dwells within me...
I see in my members another law
at war with the law of my mind...
Wretched man that I am!
Who will deliver me from this body of death?

Romans 7: 15–24

Religion, Freud believed, only hindered this healing process by keeping people infantile. God is no more than a projection of the human need for a father-figure, which people must reject in order to become adults.

(On the other hand) the suggestion that the idea of a personal God is a product of wishful thinking is quite as consistent with the belief that there is a personal God as with the belief that there isn't. Men's wishes may certainly deceive them... but they may also lead them to what is there. The wish to believe in God may be like a plant stretching out its tendrils to water. If that happens, it is because water exists; it is not evidence that the existence of water is an illusion. Admittedly, things do not exist because we desire them; but from the fact that we desire them it does not follow that they do not exist.

A. Vidler, *Christian Belief*

Carl Jung 1875–1961

Carl Jung agreed with his one-time colleague Freud in many respects. For him, as for

Freud, God was not an objective reality, but a projection of the human mind. How could it be otherwise if God by definition transcends all human thinking? But Jung remained open to the existence of a God beyond this.

His conclusions, therefore, were less hostile to religion than Freud's. Far from infantilizing people, religion (like art and literature and music) has always and in all cultures fortified them, fulfilled their deepest needs, and healed their brokeness through its unifying ritual and symbols. The unconscious conflict in all humans, between conscience and instinct, between reality and fantasy, is not as unresolvable as Freud has pessimistically concluded. It is essential for life. It is only by painfully living through such conflict that growth can take place. Our divided selves have to be re-integrated again and again into a higher synthesis where life is lived more fully. In this process, religion plays an essential part, as a psychological necessity. Far from being expendable, it has to be taken very seriously indeed.

Even this 'rescue operation' of Jung's, however, was unable to limit the damage inflicted on a 'God-out-there' by Freud's psychoanalysis. He had given people an entirely new self-understanding, and it would take years for religion to come to terms with it.

For discussion
Freud reckoned that his branch of science (psychology) had a more devastating effect on our understanding of ourselves than either cosmology (Galileo) or anthropology (Darwin). Do you agree?

Pierre Teilhard de Chardin 1881–1955

Born into a French family of eleven, Teilhard de Chardin studied for the Jesuit priesthood and was ordained in 1911. He was decorated for bravery in World War I, after which his interest in geology took him to China,

Siberia, Africa and the USA, where he died. He is famous for outlining a credible theory whereby evolution, far from destroying a religious interpretation of the world, actually confirms it.

Teilhard de Chardin agreed with Marx that what is basic and primary about our universe is matter, which evolves into more and more complex structures. In **biogenesis**, matter becomes living, and life eventually becomes aware of itself in **noogenesis** (mind). This is best illustrated in the appearance of humans (**anthropogenesis),** whose wondrous complexity and permanence suggests that this was no fluke, but the end purpose of the evolution of matter.

Among humans, finally, Teilhard de Chardin saw the emergence of Christ (**Christogenesis**) as revealing the meaning of the whole process. For Christ points to God, who is not to be thought of as working from the outside, but as the organic centre giving unity to the process. All those who have been incorporated into Christ form a spearhead pointing to a higher stage which still lies in the future, when humans will find total solidarity, unanimity and harmony.

Teilhard de Chardin called this final stage the **Theosphere** or **Omega Point**, and saw it as already existing, drawing the whole of creation to its future consummation. The creative activity of God, far from being abolished by the theory of evolution, is shown to be more breathtakingly marvellous than we had ever thought.

I believe the universe is an evolution;
I believe evolution is towards spirit;
I believe spirit is completed, in human
beings, in the personal;
I believe the supreme personal is the
Universal Christ.
If, as a result of some interior revolution,
I were successively to lose my faith in Christ,
my faith in a personal God,
my faith in the Spirit,
I think that I would still continue to believe
in the world.

The world (the value, the infallibility, the
goodness of the world)
that, in the final analysis,
is the first and last thing in which I believe.
It is by this faith that I believe.
It is by this faith that I live,
and it is to this faith, I feel,
that at the moment of death, mastering all
doubts,
I shall surrender myself.
I surrender myself to this undefined faith
in a single and Infallible World,
wherever it may lead me.

P. Teilhard de Chardin,
The Teilhard Review

Many find parts of Teilhard de Chardin's thinking naïve. Indeed since he was forbidden by his religious superiors to publish any of his ideas until after his death, he was never able to benefit from the constructive criticism of other scientists and theologians. This is not to belittle his noble attempt to break through the squabbles between science, philosophy, theology and mysticism, and bind them into a poetic whole. It can only be admired.

When he was asked to condemn the writings of Teilhard de Chardin, Pope Pius XII (1871–1958) said, 'One Galileo in 2000 years is enough.'

For discussion
Both scientists and theologians find Teilhard de Chardin a bit of an embarrassment. Are they both right? Or both wrong?

THE ORIGIN OF THE UNIVERSE

WHERE science and religion are going to clash most violently, it would seem, is in their understanding of the origin of the universe. The religious picture outlined in the opening chapters of the Bible differs so strongly and in so many respects from the picture in the mind of most modern scientists, that any agreement would seem to be out of the question.

The scientific picture

Until quite recently, after years of astrophysical research, scientists investigating the origin of the universe had agreed upon what was known as the theory of '**Continuous Creation**' or '**Steady State**'. According to this theory, the overall density of the universe has always remained constant. The fact that its galaxies have always expanded and still do so is to be explained by the continued creation of new matter.

This theory was finally abandoned in the 1960s, after the American astronomer Edwin Hubble (1889–1953) had published the results of his observation of cosmic radiation. Hubble's findings suggest that the continued expansion of the universe can be traced back to a single 'creation event' – the explosion of a phenomenally dense nucleus of matter 15,000 million years ago. The origin of this nucleus and the cause of the 'Big Bang' remain a mystery. It is presumed that the process will eventually be reversed and at some cosmically distant point in the future will lead to a 'Big Crunch'.

The initial explosion formed an immense number of hot stars hurtling from the centre. 5000 million years ago, a particularly large one (a **supernova**) itself exploded and formed a galaxy (among 500 million other galaxies) composed of 100,000 million smaller stars. The sun is one of these stars and Planet Earth is one of its relatively new cooled-down satellites.

As it cooled, earth was covered with a liquid layer of various chemicals (hydrogen, ammonia, methane, nitrogen, carbon dioxide). Through evaporation, radioactivity and the heat of the sun, these simple molecules evolved into more complex proteins and acids, which eventually became able to reproduce themselves. This first form of life, most rudimentary, seems to have occurred about 4000 million years ago.

These figures are literally astronomical and also impossible to fathom. They can be cross-checked to some extent by counting tree rings (which give dates up to 8000 years ago), by stratified fossils (the Grand Canyon in Arizona offers strata one mile in depth), and by measuring the radiation of one-time living beings, and comparing it with the radiation of uranium and potassium (which give dates of millions of years).

For discussion

Talk of 'creation' is ambiguous. It suggests a single act from which the creator can then retire. This may be true of a 'created' artefact, but a created *universe* has no more intrinsic reason to continue existing than it has to appear in the first place. Is genuine creation necessarily a continuous activity?

The biblical picture

The Bible paints a very different picture of the origins of the world. The process, far from extending over countless millennia, is completed within six days. The primeval darkness is dispelled by the creation of light, and the primeval waters are divided first by the creation of solid sky (rain above and seas below) and then by amassing the seas in order to allow the underlying dry land to appear, already clothed in vegetation.

The sun, moon and stars only come on to the scene in the second half of the week, which comes to a climax with the appearance (in already distinct species) of birds, sea creatures, land animals and finally humans (see Genesis 1: 1 – 2: 4).

The lifetime of the universe compressed into a year

Jan	1	Big Bang	15,000 million years ago
Feb			
Mar			
Apr			
May			
Jun			
Jul			
Aug			
Sep	1	Formation of the solar system	5000 million years ago
	15	Planet Earth emerges	4500 million years ago
	30	Earliest life forms appear	4000 million years ago
Oct			
Nov			
Dec	15	Worms evolve	600 million years ago
	24	Dinosaurs roam the earth	300 million years ago
	31	10.30 p.m. First humans appear	2.5 million years ago

Not only is this creation completed within days, but its starting point is, as it were, within striking distance – only 6000 years ago. The Irish Archbishop Ussher in 1650 gathered together all the ages of the patriarchal ancestors of King David (1000 BCE), and calculated that the Bible presumes Adam and Eve to have been created in October 4004 BCE.

The contrast between this and the scientific account scarcely needs spelling out. The universe is not the chance outcome of blind and random forces, but the carefully designed masterpiece of a purposive Creator. The earth is not an insignificant speck of stardust milling around among millions of others, but so central to the universe that all the rest of the heavenly bodies are subservient to it. Humans are not simply more sophisticated animals, they breathe with the very spirit of God because they are the result of a distinct and special act of creation (Genesis 2: 7). Nor do humans ascend upwards from apes. Endowed with a freedom enjoyed by no animal, they have descended downwards ever since Adam (Genesis 3: 6).

Can these differences be resolved?

There are three possible answers to this question.

a *No.* The supporters of Creationism (or Fixism) hold that since the Bible is the inerrant Word of God, its account of origins must be upheld and the evolutionary picture offered by science repudiated. The account in the book of Genesis is to be taken quite literally. Planet Earth *does* stand at the centre of a comparatively young universe and if this does not seem to square with the fossil record one can only conclude that God planted the fossils in the rocks (and created trees with concentric rings already inside them) to test people's faith.

b *No.* The Bible's claim to offer divinely revealed information is a fraud. Science has shown it to be wrong on all manner of things, not least on the origin of the universe. This means that the whole book is suspect and it should be rejected as a piece of primitive literature, containing nothing by myths, fantasies and wishful thinking.

c *Yes.* The Word of God written in Scripture presumably does not contradict the Word of God written in the rocks. Both must be treated with respect, and interpreted with care.

The biblical and scientific accounts of our origins will conflict with each other only if they are read as alternatives, of which one is true and the other false. But they can *both* be true, in their own distinct way. Science tells us the 'how' of the matter, and does it very well. The Bible is concerned with the deeper question of 'why'.

The author of Genesis is obviously not trying to tell *how* the universe came to be. There is no way he could have known. But what he could tell was his belief that the universe *as he saw it* was the work (whether directly or indirectly) of a God of power and love.

To the unscientific observer the earth is a flat disc, covered with a solid dome which separates the heavenly and the subterranean waters. Across the dome moves the small sun, the smaller moon and the tiny stars.

This simple world-view is no more than a framework. The ancient Egyptians and Babylonians used a similar framework – they had no other. But the author of Genesis uses the framework to profess his faith in the one God from whom such a world comes and for whom it exists. He passionately believes in the fundamental goodness (seven times repeated, like a litany) of such a world, and in the nobility of humans as the beneficiaries and guardians of such a world.

Whenever and however the universe came into existence, there is no reason why this profession of faith of a religious person should not be reconciled with the understanding of a scientist.

For discussion

How satisfying do you find this attempt to reconcile religion and science?

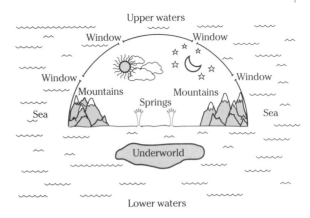

The world according to Genesis

The first man appeared on the fifth day, falling out of a pea-pod on to the soft earth. The Raven, who had created the pea-pod, gave him berries to eat, in order to make more berries grow. Then the Raven made mountain sheep out of clay, and flapped his wings to bring them to life. Then more animals and fish and birds to delight the man. But seeing that the man was lonely, he made another clay figure like the man, and fastened watercress upon its head for hair, and flapped his wings to bring her to life. 'This is your helper and your mate', he said. The man loved her, and they soon had a child. And people and animals grew and thrived and filled the earth.

Eskimo myth

The Creator God emerged from the nothingness of the universal egg, and lived for 18,000 years. He separated the yang-sky from the yin-earth, and filled the space between. He chiselled out rivers, scooped out valleys and oceans, and piled up mountains. He put stars and moon into the night sky, and the sun into the day. When he died, his skull became the dome of the sky, his body became the soil, his bones the rocks, and his blood the rivers and seas. His voice produced the thunder, his breath the winds, his sweat the rain, his hair plant life, and the fleas in his hair human beings. Then pain and suffering began.

Chinese myth, 600 BCE

In the beginning, God made the birds, the animals and the fishes. Then he made man, who copied everything that God did – sawing wood, forging iron, and so on. But when the man began to kill animals, God expelled him for a time. Then the man's pot broke, his dog died, and even his own son. He went to God to complain, and found God had restored them all as good as new. He asked to share these powers, but God refused. God moved away across the river, but the man made a raft and followed him. God made a mountain and settled on top if it, but the man climbed up and reached him. A spider advised God to go and live in the sky, and made him thread to get there, where he vanished from man's sight. The man chopped down trees, and piled log on log to climb up to the sky, but the pile collapsed. From then on, the only contact man had with God was the daily sunrise, which he continues to greet with the words, 'Our God has come.'

Myth from Zambia

For discussion

These stories seem to have grown up without any dependence on the Bible stories of creation. Point out the similarities and differences. How would you explain these?

RECONCILING RELIGION AND SCIENCE

THE origin of the universe has become famous as an area where religion and science have fought many bitter battles. But it is not the only one. Science and religion have found themselves at odds over and over again, in many different areas, as we have repeatedly seen in the section 'Great names in science' (pages 68–76). What are the hopes of a real and lasting reconciliation between them? Several different solutions have been offered.

Concordism

Some religious people have tried to make peace with science by 'discovering' texts in the Bible that not only concord with science, but actually anticipate it. Surely the primacy given to the creation of light in Genesis 1:3 is a reference to the Big Bang? Surely the emergence of the earth from a 'formless chaos' reveals an understanding of its original gaseous state? Surely the naming of the first human as Adam ('earth') shows knowledge of his evolution from matter? And surely the six 'days' of creation refer to the six great geological eras into which scientists later divided the history of the universe?

It is not only Genesis that has received this treatment. Prophets, psalms, gospels, epistles – all are scoured to find occasional texts that are unexpectedly but quite miraculously found to fit in exactly with recent scientific discoveries.

The 'solution' is both naïve and dishonest. Naïve because it would confer a science degree on the biblical authors for having stumbled on scientific truths which none of their readers would understand until the 20th century. Dishonest because, while flaunting the few texts which seem to concord with science, it conveniently says nothing about the countless other texts which quite innocently are in blatant discord with the findings of modern science.

A stopgap God

Some religious people try to make room for science by acknowledging all the dark areas on which it has shed light, but claiming that there are other areas which remain a mystery. In the course of human history, these areas have obviously become fewer (earthquakes, volcanoes, storms, etc., are now seen as natural, not as supernatural) but there will always be a gap between what we actually know and all that there is to be known. This gap is where God lives.

Barring a few high-spirited miracles long ago, the one thing God seems to avoid is interfering with his original design. I never had any trouble with the conflict between creation and Darwin after a nun explained to me that God – having the advantage of omniscience – had simply set up various mechanisms, starting with the Big Bang or protoplasm or whatever, knowing how they would evolve and select.

She was all in favour of scientists because 'they explore the mind of God through his wonderful inventions. Isn't that grand?' When I asked her whether cancer and heart attacks and her own arthritis were grand, she serenely said, 'It's all part of the big plot. They're problems that he sets us, to see how we get on. He's a very interesting person, God. Don't you think?'

Libby Purvess,
The Tablet, October 1999

This solution has become more popular since science has become more humble and hesitant than it used to be, conscious of how mysterious our universe still remains. It is far more random and unpredictable than was once thought, made up of 'impulses' rather than 'building blocks', evolving in sudden steps rather than in a steady incline and exhibiting chaos as well as clockwork regularity (see page 19). There is much about our world which remains dark and hidden – plenty of room for God!

This more reverent view of the universe has received a great boost with the recent discovery of the 'anthropic principle'. According to this, the cosmos is human-shaped because it was orientated in that direction from the very first instant of the Big Bang. Every stage in its evolution was so finely tuned that the slightest variation in the forces involved would have produced a sterile world. This argues to a purposive Designer (see page 18).

But perhaps such a God is too small. Will not a God who inhabits only the dark areas of our knowledge continue to be edged out,

inch by inch, as further research (in physics, biology, genetics, psychology, etc.) illuminates them? What if we discover that there were several Big Bangs?

A new concept of God

The advances made by science over recent centuries have so dented the traditional understanding of God that, unless a new concept of God is found, religion will be more and more discarded as a total irrelevance in a scientific world.

Clearly the *deistic* God who once wound up the clock and retired is no longer appropriate. Neither is the *theistic* God who lives in another world and occasionally intervenes in ours. Nor is the *stopgap* God who dies off by inches as his mysteries are invaded.

Theologians today talk of a *panentheistic* God, who is not outside the universe since the universe is *in* such a God. This God is no longer to be thought of as some remote 'Thing', but as an empowering ideal at the heart of things, at once the ground on which the universe is based, and the goal towards which it is directed.

This is the kind of God that the disciples saw embodied in the life of Jesus – in which they experienced a love which suffers yet never lets go, and which served as the ultimate assurance that evil will be overcome. Christians believe that such a love even now penetrates the whole universe, which will reach its final purpose in a community where each undertakes responsibility for the other.

In such a universe, the parts cannot be understood except in the context of the whole, and in the context of the goal towards which the universe is in process.

Two languages

In order to be reconciled with science, religious people do not only need a new concept of God. They also need to be aware that, although they use the same language as scientists, they mean something quite different. The religious statement 'God is in the heavens' is totally different from the scientific statement 'The stars are in the heavens.'

Humans have always in fact used language in two different ways. In one way they write recipes, order the milk, or ask the way to the shops. Here the language is as clear, accurate and precise as possible. But there are things in life which cannot be expressed so precisely – hopes and fears, faith and fantasies – and here one can only speak approximately, 'as if', in metaphors and by analogy.

The scientist can measure a page and the thickness of the paper, count the number of lines, and specify the ink that is used on it. The believer is primarily interested in the meaning of the poem written on the paper. Science looks for factual answers, and because these are limited, it is highly successful. Religion always looks deeper and has often had to break the bounds of language in order to express what it has found.

Both ways of using the language are necessary. But the language used by one is neither equivalent to the language used by the other, nor interchangeable with it. The two statements, 'Your eyes shine like the stars' and 'The light of the stars can be measured in millions of kilowatts', can *both* be true.

Dialogue

Lasting reconciliation between religion and science demands more than a recognition of differences in language. There must be real dialogue. Each must listen to the other with deep respect, so that what one has to say may positively complement the other, instead of being simply negative.

The world which science explores *is* the only world there is – which, for believers, means God's world. For believers, therefore, the revelations of science speak of God as clearly as the Word of God in the sacred books of religion. And the 'miracles' it produces, for example in medicine, should be greeted with as great awe and joy as the miracles of which the Gospel tells.

Happily we have survived into a day when science and theology no longer speak to each other in the language of fishmongers...

Scientists and theologians have learned a healthy respect for each other and for the methods employed in each field. We have learned that the question of cosmic origins does not cease to be a religious question because it has become a scientific question. We know that earlier generations were wrong when they employed the Bible as a pseudo-scientific source; but let us not think too hardly of them, they could not have known better. We know that science can neither assert nor deny the answer to the religious question, because science cannot go beyond the level of the phenomena which it observes. Science must still begin with a void and empty waste over which darkness broods. No matter how far back science pushes its investigations, no matter what it finds before that empty waste, it will never reach the level of the first chapter of Genesis.

J. L. McKenzie, *The Two Edged Sword*

Despite continual mutual mistrust, the relationship between religion and science has slowly improved towards a new openness. The trend is most striking with physicists. Many today see the inadequacy of the materialistic-positivistic world-view and understanding of reality, and also the relativity of their methods. Particularly among the physicists, we now find very few militant atheists. The invention of the atom bomb... and the negative consequences of scientific and technical progress... have raised the question of responsibility, and consequently the question of ethics, of meaning, of a scale of values, of models, and of religion.

Hans Küng, *Does God Exist?*

Science without religion is handicapped. Religion without science is blind.

Albert Einstein (1879–1955)

Sometimes people ask if religion and science are opposed to each other. They are: in the sense that the thumb and fingers of my hand are opposed to one another. It is an opposition by means of which anything can be grasped.

Prof. Sir William Bragg (1890–1971)

Science can purify religion from error and superstition. Religion can purify science from idolatry and false absolutes.

Pope John Paul II

The Science versus Religion match is usually conducted most loudly by people who would benefit from a few months reading a third discipline – philosophy.

A. Wilson, *God's Funeral*, p. 202, John Murray 1999

SAMPLE EXAM QUESTIONS

1 Describe the major differences which may exist between a scientific and a religious account of the origins of the universe. How far may these two types of accounts be compatible with each other?

(Edexcel AS sample paper)

2 Explain and evaluate the view that science has replaced God when it comes to understanding the origins of the universe.

(AQA AS sample paper)

3 How convincing are Creationist answers to Darwinism?

(OCR AS and A sample paper)

4 How fair is the comment that biblical accounts of the origin of the world have nothing useful to say to people today?

(OCR AS and A sample paper)

5 To what extent have the theories of modern scientists about the origin of the universe strengthened the case for the existence of God?

(OCR A sample paper)

6 To what extent can it be argued that the discoveries of modern scientists have produced evidence against the existence of God?

(OCR A sample paper) (essay)

The atomic bomb

For discussion

Does science need religion more than religion needs science?

7 God and miracles

The discussion of miracles is a peculiarly Christian exercise. Not that miraculous happenings are absent from the literature of other religions. But there they are marginal, and often legendary. In schoolbooks about Judaism, for example, the subject is not even mentioned in the index. There are plenty of Muslim stories attributing miracles to Muhammad, but they all come from times later than the Prophet himself, who pointed to the Qur'an as the supreme miracle, obviating the need for any other.

> *Non-believers say 'Unless he works a miracle, we will not believe.' Tell them you are commissioned to be a preacher only, not a miracle-worker.*
>
> Qur'an, Surah 13

For Christians, however, the miracles spoken of in the Gospels have become (at least in their later history) of prime importance. Many see them as Christianity's foundational credentials. Upon their authenticity, Christianity stands or falls.

THE MIRACULOUS ▬

ONE of the difficulties about discussing miracles (whether biblical ones or those reported as happening in our own time) is that there is no agreement about what the word should mean. What counts as a miracle?

When the word is used in a book of theology, it has overtones of a divine conjuring trick: something which is impossible, which breaks the laws of nature, which surpasses the power of nature and so is 'super-natural'. But why imagine that nature is bound by laws, or that we can dictate what nature is capable of? On the other hand, when the word 'miracle' appears in the daily papers, it means nothing more than something surprising, wondrous, awesome or new. A remarkable recovery from illness, or a lucky escape from disaster, or some surprising stroke of good fortune, even a last-minute winning goal is dubbed 'miraculous'. And so is the everyday event of the birth of a baby. Ask any mother.

It is interesting that the word 'miracle' continues, in most people's mind, to have this secular and earthbound sense. It is strange, therefore, that theologians should ever have tried to give the word a totally ethereal and otherworldly meaning. For them, a miracle was not a miracle unless it contravened the laws of nature. Nature was governed by fixed and iron laws, and these laws had to be violated or suspended before one could talk of miracles. A miracle was the inexplicable, the 'impossible'. Water had to run uphill before it could be recognized as the handwriting of God.

This theology was based on a view of nature which only became popular in the 18th century, and has already been abandoned by most scientists. Today's scientists no longer speak of laws, only of hypotheses which fit the facts, and which need to be tested over and over again. Since Einstein discovered relativity, and Rutherford the nucleus of the atom, and Bohr the quantum theory, we have lived in a universe of constant surprises. Each surprise has made us reassess the mysterious world we live in. No one imagines that there are no further surprises in the pipeline. But these will only make us readjust our hypotheses again, so that they fit and explain the newly discovered facts. No facts are regarded as inexplicable.

It is important to realize that the Bible uses the word 'miracle' in this worldly sense, not in the otherworldly sense. What is acclaimed as a miracle is anything which reveals the God of surprises, whether it is the star-spangled sky proclaiming the glory of God, or a simple blade of grass which speaks to the believer of God's power.

Miracles and Jesus

The Gospel story of Jesus is filled with examples of his remarkable healing powers. No scholar imagines that these are fiction. Remove the healing stories and the whole Gospel falls to pieces. On the other hand, no one any longer pretends that Jesus was unique in this regard. Healers have existed throughout history, in all cultures, even atheistic ones. Could it be that all humans possess psychosomatic powers which very few avail themselves of? Jesus was quite certainly a healer, but to call his healing work 'miraculous' tells us (in itself) nothing.

Strangely, the Gospel texts suggest that Jesus himself had considerable reservations about these healing powers – they could mean different things to different people. He rebuked those who only came to gape, just as Paul later accused miracle-seekers of immaturity and lack of faith. To demand that God must 'present his credentials' before he can be accepted is materialism of the grossest kind.

Jesus said (to the royal official), *'Unless you see signs and wonders you will not believe!'*

John 4:48

An evil and adulterous generation seeks for a sign (miracle), *but no sign shall be given to it.*

Matthew 12:39

Many will say to me, 'Lord, Lord, did we not…do many mighty works in your name?' And then will I declare to them, 'I never knew you; depart from me, you evildoers.'

Matthew 2:22–3

Brethren, do not be children in your thinking… (Speaking miraculously in) tongues is a sign not for believers but for unbelievers.

1 Corinthians 14:20–2

Jesus' teaching has nothing to do with miracles. If his mission had been simply to demonstrate a new method of restoring lost eyesight, the miracle of curing the blind would have been entirely relevant. But to say, 'You should love your enemies, and to convince you of this, I will now proceed to cure this gentleman of a cataract', would have been, to a man of Jesus' intelligence, the proposition of an idiot.

George Bernard Shaw (1856–1950)

Miracles as signs

Because wonders can be misinterpreted, Jesus took care to offer his own interpretation. For him, the healings accompanying his preaching were signs that God's Supreme Rule was being established in a godless world. The wounded human race was beginning to be restored to wholeness and health.

If it is by the Spirit of God that I cast out demons, then the Kingdom of God has come upon you.

Matthew 12:28

He thought it important that people should grasp this meaning. The wonders he worked were only signposts pointing to that meaning, and he did not want people continuing to stare at the signposts. He intended people to ask whether their own blindness was being lifted, their own paralysis overcome, their own lives fulfilled and made whole.

It is the Fourth Gospel which puts most emphasis on the symbolic value of the miracle stories of Jesus. For the author, each of the miracles he recounts is a 'sign', that is to say, a significant event, full of meaning. What the reader must look for, therefore, is not the nuts and bolts of the event ('How did he do it?') but what it means. The event, however it may have registered on the Richter scale of history, points beyond itself to something far more important. And in each case, the 'beyond' that is being pointed to is the death of Jesus, where the glory of God will be manifested as never before. For the author, the cross of Jesus is the wonder of all wonders, the ultimate revelation that God's power is the power of love.

So the story of the wedding at Cana (John 2) becomes a parable of the God who is wedded to the human race in the person of Jesus, whose death and resurrection 'on the third day' transformed the old and ineffectual into the new and lifegiving, a transformation which is commemorated in the drinking of the eucharistic wine. Similarly, the story of the food on the hillside at Passover time (John 6) is a preview of the Passover when Jesus was to climb the hill of Calvary, and satisfy the hunger of countless thousands from the human nothingness of a dead body, to be acclaimed by believers as the Promised One. The story of the walking on the water (also in John 6) evokes the resurrection narrative, in which a Jesus whom the waters of death have not been able to master reassures his disciples that it is he, not a ghost from the underworld, who is still present with them. The story of the curing of the blind (John 9) concerns not just one Jerusalem beggar in the first century but all men and women, born into darkness but enlightened by the one sent from above (Siloam), as they allow the water or Spirit of his crucified body to wash over them. The story of Lazarus (John 11) is more than the resuscitation of a friend: it too is a parable of all who hear the voice of God in the crucified Jesus, and respond to it as he calls them out of a living death into a life that is like God's, eternal.

Set out in a single paragraph, this short analysis of the Fourth Gospel may appear unconvincing. Can stories as simple as these bear the weight of such profound theology? Those unfamiliar with the Gospel of John need to be reassured. All Johannine scholars are agreed that John's use of symbolism, allusion and cross-reference is highly sophisticated, and quite deliberate. All his stories, especially those of miracles, point to the God whose true nature, he claims, is revealed in the death of Jesus.

WHAT REALLY HAPPENED?

I F John gives such a strong theological slant to his miracle stories, what is to prevent the other three evangelists doing the same? Presumably nothing. It is true that John has always been called 'The Theologian', with the implication that the other three were little more than 'The Historians'. But present scholarship insists that Matthew and Luke, even the 'original' Mark, are quite as determined as John to present a particular interpretation of Jesus, not simply to record the bare historical facts. And the miracle stories they relate will inevitably be coloured by such interpretation.

This means, of course, that the actual historical reality standing behind the miracle stories is now lost to us. It is impossible to reconstruct the original photographable event, simply because we only have access to it through the eyes of those who have already imposed their interpretation on it. Was the story of Cana in John 2 originally a parable Jesus told rather than an event in which he took part? Was the feeding of the multitudes in Mark 6 originally only a token meal, of which the details later became exaggerated? Was the raising of the widow's son in Naim (Luke 7) originally embroidered from the similar story in 2 Kings 4 based on nearby Shunem, in order to show Jesus as even greater than Elisha?

No one can answer such questions. Nor is it important, given the emphasis of the storytellers, that such questions should receive a definite yes or no. After all, which is more telling or more worthwhile: incontrovertible evidence that Jesus did actually walk on water, or a story which expresses the faith of Jesus' disciples, that in him they experienced the invincible power of God. 'That man? He could walk on water!'

If a science teacher gives his pupil a flower, the question he asks is, 'What is this?' If the pupil is later given the same flower by her boyfriend, the question that is asked is, 'What does this mean?' The precise botanical species of the flower is no longer relevant. In something of the same way, the historical reality of Jesus's miracles – What Really Happened? – is irrelevant to the evangelist. The further we probe into that aspect of them, the further we remove ourselves from his only interest.

Explaining the miracles away?

Is such a treatment of the Gospel miracles too cavalier? They once told us forcefully and unambiguously who Jesus was. Do they now tell us nothing? Are they now so demoted and diluted as to be worthless? Have they simply been explained away? Parables, poetry, symbolism – is this all that is left? Of what use is that to serious readers of the Gospel?

It depends what serious readers are looking for. If it distresses them to acknowledge poetry as poetry, if they are unaware that poetry can get nearer to the heart of truth than a mere recital of bald facts, then perhaps they are less serious than they imagine. If someone told you that your eyes shone like the stars, would you start asking questions about kilowatts?

The approach that has been outlined above does not aim to get rid of the miracles, but to understand them. It aims to restore a more biblical image of God, whose saving power is to be seen in what is natural, not in what is unnatural. It aims above all to reinstate Jesus of Nazareth as a human being, a man among men, not a

Superman. Jesus was a human being, and could do no more than any other human being fired by the Spirit of God can do. Yet in what he did, his disciples confessed that they had seen the glory of God present among them.

Did the 'impossible' take place? The answer is that this central claim of the Christian Gospel is itself 'impossible' – that the Word of God became flesh and dwelt among us, that God was in Christ reconciling the world to himself. If anyone believes in that central 'impossibility', then it is rather pointless to keep asking questions about the historical accuracy of the miracle stories. It is rather as if the woman arrested for adultery (see John 8: 1–11), having been sent away pardoned, could only remark on the fact that Jesus was wearing sandals at the time.

Jesus worked miracles, but since he was a human being they were the kind of miracles that human beings can work. And so he presumed, quite naturally, that his disciples would work miracles greater than this own:

Truly, truly, I say to you
he who believes in me
will also do the works that I do;
and greater works than these will he do.

John 14: 12

God is not 'Lord-over-us', but 'Strength-in-us'.
The miracles of Jesus are not distinct from ours; we too drive out demons and heal the sick.

Dorothee Sölle, *Celebrating Resistance*

After all, would they not, under the inspiration of the Spirit he breathed out as he died, be able to feed the hungry and expel demons that haunt the human race, to heal the sick and offer new life to people, in far greater numbers than he could ever hope to help in his own mortal lifetime? This is not 'explaining the miracles away'. It is an invitation to understand them more deeply, and to accept a frightening responsibility: we are, each of us, called to work miracles ourselves.

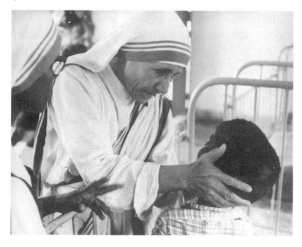

We too heal the sick

THE THEOLOGY OF MIRACLES

GOD-TALK is often presented as if it refers to a Superperson living in a world of his own, occasionally intervening in this world of men and women to remind them that he is around, even if he is largely absent. Many people have sensibly rejected such a God. The true Jewish and Christian tradition speaks of a God who is present in history and can only be known in the events of people's lives. There is only one world, not two, and God is present at the heart of it.

Christ-talk is more often than not tinged with this double-think. Jesus is presented as someone from outer space, and his humanity is a fraud. This is also something most sensible people find impossible to take – and rightly so. Jesus was as human as any of his disciples, and incapable of working any miracles they could not work.

Gospel-talk is often clumsily presented as if it referred to a straightforward historical narrative, of which all the statements were to be taken as a simple piece of objective reporting. This not only puts people off, but is at variance with what anyone who has studied the texts knows to be the case. The texts present Jesus in the way a believer now sees him, not in the way his contemporaries then saw him. The miracle stories are part of this statement of faith.

The one event in Jesus' life which made the authors of the Gospels use such high-flown language about him was not this miracle or that, but his death. It was in that event, and in their reflective understanding of it, that they saw Jesus as the clearest revelation yet given of what God is really like, in terms of love, forgiveness and acceptance. Each of the Gospel miracle stories is meant to evoke that final insight.

Conclusion

What has been said above more or less bypasses the classical objection to miracles, especially those eloquently put by the Scottish philosopher David Hume (1711–76). Having defined miracles as violations of the laws of nature, he argued that, if it is reasonable to proportion one's belief to the evidence available, then the overwhelming evidence of our own experience (where water does not change into wine, nor people walk on water, nor the dead come back to life) puts miracles very low in the order of probability. If, moreover, the evidence offered is shoddy, then their credibility grows even less. The Gospel miracles in particular, he says, are reported by unreliable, gullible, primitive and prejudiced witnesses, ignorant of science, prone to superstition and enamoured of fantasy. He concludes that it will always be more rational to believe that the laws of nature continue to hold, than that these outlandish stories should be taken seriously. They are obvious cases of coincidence or exaggeration, of misinterpretation or wish-fulfilment.

No testimony is sufficient to establish a miracle, unless the testimony be of such a kind that its falsehood would be more miraculous than the fact which it endeavours to establish... There is not to be found, in all history, any miracle attested

One could put further objections. It would seem strange that a Creator God should construct a world so clumsy that it needs constant readjustment on behalf of his friends. It would seem strange that these divine interventions should concern trivialities like providing wine at a wedding or healing a sick person at Lourdes, but not be in the least bothered by such disasters as Auschwitz or Hiroshima. And it would seem strange to make God responsible for the miracles on which half a dozen conflicting religions base their claims, and which effectively cancel each other out.

These objections are powerful and cannot be glibly dismissed. On the other hand, they depend almost entirely on an understanding of nature as being regulated by rigid laws, which can be breached only by divine intervention. There are very few people today (least of all scientists) who see our world in these terms. Nature continues to produce surprises, not only for believers but for unbelievers too, and they are as 'natural' as the day-to-day activities of nature. No one any longer volunteers to predict what nature may or may not be capable of. Hume was right to point out that a superstitious interpretation of our world is irrational, but isn't a purely mechanical interpretation equally irrational?

Hume was too absolute in his judgement about miracles. A reverent **agnosticism** would seem more appropriate. Certainly, as far as the Gospel miracles are concerned, we are no longer in a position to reconstruct exactly what took place. Once grapes have been transformed into wine, it is impossible to reconstruct them back into grapes. Some of the miracle stories told about Jesus may be exaggerated or quite legendary, or even parables that were never meant to be taken as history. Christians continue to revere the stories because they speak of the power of Christ, and because what they *mean* is far more important to Christians than what actually happened.

God is really on the inside, we must find him in the processes, not in the gaps. We know now there are no gaps, no points at which a special intervention is conceivable. From first to last the process has been continuous. Nature is all of a piece, a seamless robe. There is no evidence of a break, as we once imagined, between inorganic matter and the emergence of the first living organisms; nor between man's animal precursors and the emergence of man himself. If the hand of God is to be recognized in this continuous creation, it must be found not in isolated intrusions, not in any gaps, but in the very process itself.

J. V. Taylor, *The Go-Between God*, SCM

Nature is not a closed definable system. The new takes place again and again... The ordinary events of life are not simply due to the unfolding of fixed laws, but the result of God's redemptive presence in human life, and hence as much surprising and gratuitous as are miracles... Miracles are startling events that go against man's immediate expectations, but they are signs to men only if they call to mind the ever startling grace of God operative in their lives. To people who do not believe, miracles mean nothing.

Miracles are not violations of the natural order, helping us to prove the existence of a transcendent God and the loving concern he has for human life. Miracles are not even divine signs revealing the power of God and confirming the message preached in his name. Miracles are simply startling events that bring out the startling character implicit in all of human life, and hence have meaning only for those who already acknowledge the marvellous as a dimension of human history.

Gregory Baum,
Man Becoming, Herder & Herder

Miracle stories figure prominently throughout the Bible and providential answers to prayer are a characteristic feature of much popular Christian piety. In general I am unconvinced by such stories and the interpretations given of them. I do not think we are given such specific signs of God's goodness or God's power as they suggest. The New Testament's warning against dependence upon miraculous signs needs to be taken very seriously. We live by faith and not by sight. There is a hiddenness about God's goodness and his power which means that faith can never be made secure beyond a peradventure.

Maurice Wiles in *Christian Believing* (Doctrine Commission of the Church of England), SPCK 1976

Your holy hearsay
is not evidence;
give me the good news
in the present tense.

What happened
nineteen hundred years ago
may not have happened –
how am I to know?

The living truth
is what I long to see:
I cannot lean upon
what used to be.

So shut the Bible up
and show me how
the Christ you talk about
is living now.

Sydney Carter,
Nothing Fixed or Final, Galliard

For discussion

Do you believe miracles happen often, sometimes, rarely, or never? Why?

SAMPLE EXAM QUESTIONS

1 Examine the arguments which can be used to discredit belief in miracles. In what respects do you consider belief in miracles to be strong in spite of these criticisms?

(Edexcel AS sample paper)

2 'Miracle stories are an obstacle to faith for modern people.' Discuss.

(OCR A sample paper)

3 What are the major problems for modern Christians in understanding miracles?

(UCLES 1990)

4 'The Christian religion not only was at the first attended with miracles, but even at this day cannot be believed by any reasonable person without one.' (David Hume). Discuss.

(UCLES 1992)

5 The problem with miracles is not that of deciding whether they happen or not, but that of deciding what the claim 'it was a miracle' actually means. Discuss.

(NEAB 1994)

6 'A God who exists outside time is a God incapable of acting in the world.' Discuss.

(UCLES 1996)

8 *God and the 'afterlife'*

GOD-TALK AGAIN

IN the opening chapter of this book, attention was drawn to the difficulty of using religious language. 'God-talk' is so utterly different from our everyday language that it has to be used with extreme sensitivity or it will be misunderstood. To recall only one of the warnings given by theologians across the ages, Thomas Aquinas said that any statement about God, however true, will be less true than its opposite.

In this section the warning has to be repeated, and even more loudly than before. If by definition our talk about God, and our relationship with him, can only be tentative, what shall we say about talk of the afterlife. Here we enter the darkest area of our understanding of God, where philosophers of religion hardly know what questions to ask, let along what solutions to offer. People can talk from experience about some aspects of their relationship with God. But on the afterlife there is nothing to appeal to. Those who have had experience of it are not telling.

In short, there is no hard information on what happens after death, and our talk must reflect this by being hesitant and approximative. There is even less place for dogmatism here than in the rest of theology.

> *That we are here and now God's children,*
> *is something we know.*
> *What we shall be in the future*
> *we do not know:*
> *God has not revealed it to us.*
>
> 1 John 3: 2, translated by H. J. Richards

> *We don't yet know about life.*
> *How can we know about death?*
>
> Confucius
>
> (Death) – *The undiscover'd country from whose bourn*
> *No traveller returns . . .*
>
> Shakespeare, Hamlet III, 1

With no factual information to go on, is agnosticism and reverent silence the only attitude one can possibly take to this topic? Perhaps. On the other hand, while it may be true that there is nothing that we can directly *know* about the afterlife, there may be much that we can indirectly deduce, or even project. Our own present experience could be such as to allow a perfectly valid future inference to be made from it, in something of the way that a small coloured transparency can be projected on to a distant large screen. The actual reality we are considering resides in the small slide, not in the eyecatching image in the distance. Yet that image cannot be dismissed as an illusion; some projections can be firmly based in reality.

To take an example: believers speak easily of a heaven for which they yearn because there they will be eternally close to the God they love. On what do they base this idea of future bliss, having not yet experienced it? Quite simply on their present experience of God's love as an unfailing and eternal reality. What will happen when they die? They don't know. What they do know is that God has never disappointed them yet, and that therefore they can put utter confidence in the abiding presence of God, whose hands they have never failed to experience as loving ones.

> *If God is for us, who can be against us?*
> *If God has cleared us, who can call us guilty?*
> *There are no heavenly or earthly powers,*
> *there is no threat, not even death itself,*
> *that can unmake the love we've seen in Jesus.*
> *Nothing can ever take away from us*
> *the love of God that we have seen in Christ.*
>
> Romans 8:31–9,
> translated by H. J. Richards
>
> *In Paradise, I prepare for the righteous what*
> *no eye has ever seen, no ear has ever*
> *heard, and what the deepest mind could*
> *never imagine.*
>
> A saying of Muhammad

The sceptics

Belief in the afterlife is widespread, as we shall see. Nevertheless, this last century has seen an increasing number of people (especially in the West) abandoning the belief as a wild fantasy born out of fear of death and an instinct for self-preservation. In harsh reality, life is a one-off: you are born into it and you die out of it. You can no more exist after your death than you can exist before your birth.

Death is a real and final full stop, not merely a semicolon. We admit this to be the case for plants and animals – why not for humans too? Grandiose ideas about our ultimate significance, and therefore of our survival beyond death, are pitiful delusions. Indeed, once death has decomposed the human body as it decomposes other bodies, what can it possibly mean to speak of some*body* surviving? The German philosopher Ludwig Feuerbach suggested that the afterlife is simply the result of people projecting their human ideals on to an imaginary heaven. More pessimistically, Marx saw heaven as a distraction from life's misery, a useful 'opium' to numb the pain of the exploited working class. Freud fastened onto the chronic infantilism of the human race which, unable to face the real world, invents a heavenly one.

Modern science, far from challenging these pessimistic observations, has tended on the whole to confirm them. For Richard Dawkins, for example, all our 'spiritual' properties are reducible to physical ones. The human 'soul', with all its thoughts, desires and beliefs, is no more a separate entity than the 'phlogiston' of the 18th century scientists turned out to be.

> *After death you will be what you were*
> *before your birth.*
>
> Schopenhauer
>
> *The fact of having been born is a bad*
> *augury for immortality.*
>
> Santayana
>
> *Unfading moths, immortal flies,*
> *And the worm that never dies.*
> *And in that Heaven of all their wish,*
> *There shall be no more land, say fish.*
>
> Rupert Brooke, *Heaven*
>
> *Extinction. Noun. The raw material out of*
> *which theologians created the future state.*
>
> A. Bierce, *Devil's Dictionary*
>
> *How extraordinary that humans who don't*
> *know what to do with their lives should*
> *want another one which lasts for ever.*
>
> Anatole France 1844–1924

WHY AN AFTERLIFE?

*I*N the light of this summary dismissal of the afterlife as sheer fantasy, we need to ask how a belief in survival after death ever put down such firm roots in all religions and all cultures. Even the most primitive of peoples, who have left us no written records, have left evidence in their burial customs of their beliefs. Their human dead have not been disposed of as their dead animals have: they have been buried with a care and reverence which speak of the expectation of an afterlife.

The words 'all religions and all cultures' in the previous paragraph are in fact an exaggeration. A notable exception is to be found in the Israelite religion in which, from its earliest beginnings right down to New Testament times, the prospect of an afterlife played no part. People in all walks of life – patriarchs, kings, prophets, soldiers, fishermen, servants – were content to lead a deeply religious life without needing to be rewarded in another life after death.

The dead do not praise the Lord,
nor do any that go down into silence.
But we (the living) will bless the Lord
from this time forth and for evermore.

Psalm 115: 17–18

It was only in the final hundred years or so BCE, in the course of a brutal persecution, that the hope arose of a future resurrection from the dead, to allow the faithful to be rewarded in paradise, and sinners to be punished in hell. This hope was rejected as wishful thinking by many orthodox Jews (Sadducees) in the 1st century BCE, but was accepted as an article of faith by others (Pharisees). It was from this latter group that the first Christians emerged.

In spite of this important exception, it remains true, by and large, that a religious outlook on life has generally included a believe in an afterlife.

On what was this belief based? Was it a deep sense of justice and fairness which is simply not satisfied by the inequalities of life? If blatant goodness is not rewarded in the course of a lifetime, nor arrant wickedness punished, and there is no future recompense, then life becomes totally absurd. Many pages of the Hebrew Bible point this out, without drawing a clear conclusion.

Immanuel Kant developed this theme and concluded that the whole moral order of the world would collapse without an afterlife. The sense of moral obligation, which impels us to greater and greater moral holiness, cannot be fulfilled in a single lifetime.

Plato introduced the interesting distinction between body and soul. While the physical body is obviously made up of parts subject to age and corruption, it temporarily houses a spiritual 'soul' which, having no parts, is of its very nature indestructible. This is the 'real me' which will happily live for ever once it has escaped from its bodily prison.

Non omnis moriar

I shall die, but not entirely:
something of me will survive.

The Roman poet Horace,
1st century BCE, *Odes* III

Judaism never accepted such a pessimistic dualism. The body, far from being a barrier to union with God or with people, is our very lifeline to each other. We do not *have* bodies, we *are* bodies, and must be saved as bodies, or not at all. It was this line of thinking which led finally to a hope, not of the survival of the disembodied soul, but of the resurrection of the body. Both Jesus and Muhammad inherited this hope from Judaism, and bequeathed it to Christianity and Islam.

What evidence?

We have outlined some of the grounds on which religious people have based their belief in an afterlife, through reasoned argument, through inference, and through their experience of God. What can be said to people who find these arguments unconvincing and who demand evidence of a more substantial kind? Is there any hard proof that there is life beyond death?

It has been suggested that the recent study of cryonics (the deep freezing of corpses) provides ample evidence. If it also becomes possible to 'digitize' the whole of human experience, that is, to capture the total sum of a person's experiences (sight, touch, taste, smell, etc.) and record them on silicon chips, then that human experience could live on after the person's death by being played into someone else's brain. Some scientists believe we are close to achieving this rather gruesome feat. But no one imagines that this kind of 'life after death' is what religion is interested in.

The vast field of the **paranormal** is more seriously proposed as evidence that, quite independent of the physical and bodily world, there is a spirit-world immune to death. It manifests itself in **psychokinesis** (PK) where objects are moved or changed without physical contact; in telepathy, **clairvoyance** and **extrasensory perception** (ESP) where messages are transmitted from mind to mind, even at great distances; and in **near-death** or **out-of-body experiences** (OBE) where people have observed themselves, as if from afar, entering the very domain of death and returning from there. However, many of these fascinating experiences are not easily distinguishable from other strange human phenomena such as dreams, hysteria, drugged hallucinations, schizophrenia, etc. – which have their explanation in terms of medicine and psychology, and not of a spirit-world. A recent experiment by German scientists (1994) concluded that experiences similar to OBE could be created in a laboratory, and that lack of oxygen to the brain could produce the impression of visions, voices and other out-of-body experiences.

The concept of a spirit-world is better supported by the psychical research pursued over the years, the results of which may suggest the existence of another world on the far side of death, which can communicate with us by means of mediums, apparitions, automatic writing, *ouija* boards, and even the playful activity of poltergeists. But even in this well-researched area, and even when the many cases of fraud and deception have been excluded, it has not been possible to reach any indisputable conclusions. Our understanding of the human psyche, even this side of death, is still in its infancy, and much remains to be studied before it becomes clear whether the phenomena with which spiritualism

concerns itself are attached to realities this side of death, or to the beyond. Meanwhile, the alleged communications from the beyond remain rather more banal than one would have expected.

There remain two further forms of life after death which are part of the belief of a far larger number of people than the examples so far given: **immortality** and **resurrection**. Both are attempts to answer the dark question: What could life beyond death possibly consist of? If what lives on is to be really *me*, I need to know where the real me is situated. If it is in the bodily person that I am now, then my dead body will need to be restored to life. But if it is in some spiritual part that is locked inside my body, then I can happily shed that dead body in order to be free from its restrictions.

IMMORTALITY?

A S has just been mentioned, Greek philosophy, especially under the influence of Plato, opted for the second of these two alternatives. The changing material world in which we live is an illusion, the mere shadow of a world of unchanging ideas and patterns. Human spirits or souls belong to this eternal world. Pre-existing and immortal, they are for a time imprisoned in mortal bodies, from which they long to escape. This they achieve at death, when they either return to their divine origin, or are temporarily re-embodied in another form (**reincarnation** or **metempsychosis**).

Imagine a cave in which people have been shackled from birth in such a way that they cannot see the entrance but only the end wall. On the wall, all they can see [as on a TV screen?] of people passing by outside is their black and white shadows, cast by a fire beyond. One prisoner breaks free from his chains and goes out into the sunlight. Dazzled at first, it slowly dawns on him that what he has been observing all of his life is only the indistinct shadows of real humans [in full technicolor?]. He returns to tell his brothers and sisters of the real world outside, of which they have only seen two-dimensional images. They think he is mad, and kill him.

Plato, *The Republic*

Our birth is but a sleep and a forgetting;
the soul that rises with us, our life's star,
hath had elsewhere its setting
and cometh from afar:
Not in entire forgetfulness
and not in utter nakedness
but trailing clouds of glory do we come
from God who is our home.

William Wordsworth,
Intimations of Immortality

Many Christians, in spite of their talk of resurrection (see the quotations below), share the Platonic world-view: the meaning of life is to give no meaning to one's life, only to the afterlife.

Life on earth is only a single night we spend in a second-class hotel.

St Teresa of Avila

Serve the Lord. The pay isn't much, but the retirement benefits are out of this world.

Anon.

Think that no stubborne sullen Anchorit
Which fixt to a pillar, or a grave, doth sit
Bedded, and bath'd in all his ordures, dwels
So fowly as our Soules in their first-built Cels.

John Donne, *An Anatomie of the World*

But it is religions like Hinduism and Buddhism which come closest to Plato's understanding of death. Death is not to be deplored as if it were the end. It is a merciful release into a new form of life, hopefully of a higher kind. After many such purifying transmigrations, the believer hopes eventually to escape from the tyranny of separate earthly existence and to be merged and absorbed into the Eternal One.

This belief is based on both reason and evidence. Reason strongly suggests not only that our spiritual activities are quite distinct from our bodily ones, but also that the chaotic inequalities of the life into which we are born would be quite unjust if they were not a reward or a punishment for past lives. And there is evidence (slight but intriguing) for these past lives. How else are we to explain the accuracy with which some people (especially under hypnosis) can remember details of their previous existence, and even give examples of the foreign languages they once spoke?

One could ask how a new incarnation can be continuous with the old. Is a new flame lit from a dying one the same flame? Could the impression of having lived in a previous existence be traced to the subconscious memory of a story one has read, or a film one has seen? One could also ask whether a God who requires endless compensation to be paid for past misdeeds is worth worshipping. But one could add that, in spite of such criticism, more than a billion people continue to believe in reincarnation.

PLATO AND ARISTOTLE ▬

THERE have been several references above to both Plato and Aristotle. Since their thinking has had such a profound influence on philosophers throughout the centuries, and is even currently enjoying a revival, the following paragraphs may help to clarify the extent to which they agreed, or differed.

Plato (427–347 BCE) dedicated his whole life to philosophy, and finally came to the conclusion that all his thinking led to one crucial question: What is eternally (and not just momentarily) true and beautiful and good? Obviously not the world we live in! Here everything we experience is changeable. Yet the fact that everything in our world can be categorized into groups (animal, vegetable and mineral, for example) and subgroups (flies, horses, humans etc.)

Plato and Aristotle

suggests that at the head of each group there must be one perfect and unchanging pattern or archetype, of which everything in our world is an imperfect copy, a mere shadow. These universal archetypes (or 'forms' or 'ideas' as Plato calls them) are the only realities about which we can reason and have true knowledge, because they alone are permanent and unchanging.

Human souls, being immortal, are part of that unchanging world of 'ideas'. They existed there before they entered our bodies in this world, where they have forgotten the perfect world from which they came. There arc times, however, when things in our changing world remind us of the eternal archetypes we once knew, and these fill us with a longing to return, freed from our bodily prison. People who feel this are few. Fewer still do anything about it. But true philosophers ignore their body in order to see God, the paradigm of all truth and beauty and goodness.

Aristotle (384–382 BCE) was one of Plato's star pupils, and was eventually to produce systematic treatises (among other writings) on biology, education, ethics, poetry, politics and psychology. More pedestrian and down-to-earth than Plato, he had a razor sharp mind

that did not hesitate to cut through what he saw as the romanticism of his professor.

He took over the current distinction between body and soul, between matter and form, and between the senses and the intellect. But, turning Plato's thinking on its head, he concluded that it is the body, matter and senses which are primary, while soul, form and intellect exist only insofar as they 'inform' or give shape to their subject. They have no separate existence of their own, any more than the shape stamped on a piece of wax can be separated from the wax itself. There is no such thing as goodness in the abstract, only insofar as pencils or people are good. How could his professor have imagined that a game of cricket could exist without its players?

For Aristotle, therefore, the real world is not 'out there'. It is in what we see and touch and feel with our senses, without which nothing can come into the mind. The 'soul', whether of horses or humans, is no more than the engine that moves the body, and cannot be recycled when the body dies. There is no personal survival after death, since even the reason or intellect (the 'divine' in us) will lose its separate identity as it is absorbed by the eternal Unmoved Mover of the universe.

The rationalism of Aristotle was strong meat for the early Christian theologians (Augustine (354–430 CE), for example), who felt far more at ease with Plato's longing for an otherworldly solution to life's problems. This meant that Aristotle's writings were totally neglected in the West until they were rediscovered (long since translated into Arabic by Eastern mathematicians, scientists and theologians) in the 12th century. When Thomas Aquinas (1225–1274) came across them, he was fascinated by their common sense approach, and was happy to adopt their insights and make them part of his understanding of Christianity. Luther and the Protestant Reformers were deeply distrustful of Aristotle, but all Roman Catholic theology was until recently based on his philosophy as revised by Aquinas. In the Vatican Galleries, both Aristotle and Plato have become honorary Christians in Raphael's great mural, *The School of Athens* (1510).

Synonyms

Both Plato and Aristotle use more than one word to refer to the same thing (as we all do). But to confuse matters further, those who have translated their works do not agree on the precise English words to express these things. This table of synonyms might help:

Form = Idea = Model = Paradigm = Pattern = Archetype
Matter = Substance = Material = Body
Mind = Intellect = Reason
Soul = Psyche

RESURRECTION?

THE Hebrew Bible, as has already been noted, did not on the whole use Plato's dualistic language. In its thinking, it assumes what Aristotle was later to hold, that body and soul are not two separable units, but simply two dimensions of a single unity. Just as the 'team spirit' in a football side is not something distinct from the members of a team, so the spirit that gives life to a person is not separable from that person, as if it could exist in a disembodied form.

If there is an afterlife, therefore, it cannot exclude the body: a disembodied 'me' would simply no longer be 'me'. To survive death, the body must rise again from the dead. To live after death must involve a re-embodiment, or resurrection.

This way of looking at things, as we have seen, was inherited from late Judaism by the first Christians and later by Muslims. In the teaching of Jesus, there was never a shadow of doubt about the existence of an afterlife. He spoke of coming from God into the world and confidently expected to go to God at his death. His parables frequently refer to the heaven of reward or the hell of punishment that lie beyond death.

In the fourth Gospel in particular, Jesus is represented speaking of himself as the Bread of Life, and promising that those who accept him as such will be raised from the dead on the last day. St Paul in his letters repeats the same theme frequently: those who believe in Jesus will in the last analysis overcome death.

I am the Bread of Life ...
If anyone eats of this Bread
he will live for ever ...
and I will raise him up on the last day.

John 6: 48–54

I am the resurrection and the life.
He who believes in me, though he die,
yet shall he live.

John 11: 25

He who raised Christ Jesus from the dead
will give life to your mortal bodies also
through his Spirit which dwells in you.

Romans 8: 11

The trumpet will sound,
and the dead will be raised imperishable,
and we shall be changed.

1 Corinthians 15: 52

The basis of these confident assertions is, of course, the claim that Jesus himself, though he died a real death, was raised bodily from the dead by the power of God and, leaving an empty tomb behind, confirmed this fact by walking and talking and eating with his friends for weeks after. The resurrection of Jesus became such a central element of the belief of Christians that St Paul was able to say:

If Christ is not risen from the dead,
there is no Christianity.

1 Corinthians 15: 16

However, this way of looking at things also has its difficulties. If someone has only recently died (as in the story of Lazarus, or of Jesus' crucifixion), it is possible to think of a bodily resurrection as the miraculous reanimation of that person's corpse. But what if the corpse has been eaten by animals, or cremated, or simply buried for so long that it has turned to dust? In such cases, death can no longer be played down as a mere sleep, or the general resurrection (if there is to be one) thought of in terms of revivified corpses. The resurrection body, if such a thing is to exist, will need to be a new creation out of the nothingness of death.

But if that is the case, where are the dead supposed to be while they wait for this new creation? And what continuity is there between the bodies in which they died and the new resurrection bodies that they await? Why treat these risen bodies as identical to the old, if they are really only newly created replicas? What on earth (or in heaven) could such a resurrection possibly consist of? And in what way could such a mysterious postmortem existence be called bodily?

Hard questions, and made all the harder by presuming that they can be answered literally. For if (going back to the beginning again) talk of an afterlife cannot be anything other than a projection from present experience, then it obviously cannot be taken as a word-for-word description of something that can be touched and handled. All that Christians have to go on is their present experience of the love of God, as revealed in the life of Jesus. That experience compels them to say that they know such a God will not abandon them in death. They will live on 'in God'. But what this 'being in God' entails is quite unimaginable. Even Paul baulks at trying to explain. Who would ever have predicted, from the dry grains of corn thrown into a field, the glory of the wheatfield that ensues?

Someone may ask: How are dead people raised and what sort of body do they have when they come? How foolish! ... what you sow is not the body that is to be but only a bare grain of wheat. It is God who gives it the sort of body he has chosen for it.

1 Corinthians 15: 35–8,
New Jerusalem Bible

What you sow is not what you reap

Given this impossibility of describing the indescribable, believers can only turn to symbols, metaphors, parables and dramatization. The Christ who lives on after death and continues to speak to his disciples across the frontiers of death, is as surprisingly different from his previous embodiment as would be a dead body walking away from its tomb. To put it another way, if people asked where Christ was after his death, they would not be shown his tomb. That is not where his body is. He is now embodied in the community of his friends. They form the 'Body of Christ'.

Christ has no body now on earth but yours;
no hands, no feet but yours;
yours are the eyes through which
his compassion looks out on the world;
yours the feet with which he goes about
    doing good;
yours the hands with which he continues to
    bless people.

St Teresa of Avila

In the light of this, it is important to realize that the first Christians spoke of resurrection and eternal life as much in *this*-worldly language as in otherworldly language, and as much in the *present* tense as in the future tense. Neither eternal life nor resurrection is an unknown quantity reserved for those who reach the other side of death. Both are realities to be experienced here and now.

Jesus said:
He who believes in him who sent me
has eternal life . . .
and has passed from death to life

John 5:24

This is eternal life,
that they know thee, the only true God,
and Jesus Christ whom thou hast sent.

John 17:3

We have passed out of death into life,
because we love the bhrethren.

1 John 3:14

God gave us eternal life
and this life is in his Son.
He who has the Son has life.

1 John 5:11–12

Christ being raised from the dead
will never die again . . .
So you also must consider yourselves dead
to sin
and alive to God . . .
men who have been brought from death
to life.

Romans 6:9–13

By your baptism you have been raised up
with Christ . . .
You were dead . . . he has brought you to life.

Colossians 2:12–13, *New Jerusalem Bible*

If then you have been raised with Christ,
seek for the things that are above,
where Christ is.

Colossians 3:1

WHAT THE HELL AND TALK OF THE DEVIL

THE reservations that have been expressed about the meaning to be given to resurrection and eternal life must, of course, be extended to the subject of hell and the devil as well. Here too the Bible and the Qur'an use highly dramatic language. How literally should it be taken?

The New Testament references to hell are very frequent. They are to be found not only in the writings of Jesus' disciples, but in the reported teaching of Jesus himself. If he often speaks of a God of peace and love and forgiveness and heaven, he also speaks of a God of wrath and vengeance and condemnation and punishment. Many of his parables conclude on a hell which has been described as 'a lake of fire where the wicked are deep-fried for all eternity.'

He will say to those on his left hand,
'Depart from me, you cursed, into the eternal
fire prepared for the devil and his angels'.

Matthew 25:41

The Qur'an uses even stronger language:

Non-believers will be forced into fiery clothes,
and boiling water poured on them. Their skin
and entrails will melt, and they will be beaten
with iron clubs. As often as they try to escape
their torments, they will be dragged back and
told, 'Taste the pain of burning'.

Surah 22

How can these two images of God be reconciled? Perhaps they can't. Perhaps the vengeful language simply has to be dismissed as part of the pathology of religion, which always has difficulty in distinguishing its own cause from God's.

I can hardly see how anyone ought to wish
Christianity to be true; for if so, the plain
language of the text seems to show that the
men who do not believe, and this would
include my father, brother and almost all of
my best friends, will be everlastingly
punished. And this is a damnable *doctrine.*

Charles Darwin

But it is equally possible that the violent imagery should be understood as the language of enthusiasm and urgency rather than taken literally. For while it is obvious that God cannot literally be angry (love cannot be love if it is hiding a big stick for emergencies), it is equally obvious from the language that *something* is angry, namely a situation in which there is total disharmony between what is and what ought to be. Human wickedness is not a nothing, which God will dismiss with a 'There, there.' Believers claim that it is a disaster and can have nothing but destructive consequences for those who refuse to echo God's self-giving love in their lives. This does not mean that God will punish such people. But people can shipwreck their own lives. Language about hell, like language about eternal life, refers primarily to the present not to the future. The choice between heaven and hell lies before people at every moment of their lives. This choice may also be seen in the Hindu belief that the consequences of wickedness are dealt with, not by a punishing God, but by a series of purifying rebirths.

> *The New Testament statements about hell are not meant to supply information about a hereafter to satisfy curiosity and fantasy. They are meant to bring vividly before us here and now the absolute seriousness of God's claim, and the urgency of conversion in the present life. This life is the emergency we have to face.*
>
> Hans Küng, *Eternal Life?*
>
> *Only our concept of time makes it possible for us to speak of the Day of Judgement by that name. In reality it is a summary court in perpetual session.*
>
> Franz Kafka

Many of today's theologians (John Hick, for example) conclude that the eternal lovelessness of hell is a dramatic image of what the human race could achieve by its own unaided effort. But it is not a description of any sort of reality that will actually come to be, because it leaves out of the reckoning the believers' conviction that in the last analysis God is love, and that love has the power to overcome everything.

This is illustrated even in Muslims' beliefs about an eternal hell prepared for sinners:

> *If he has any goodness in his heart, even of the weight of a single barley-corn, and says, 'There is no God but Allah', he shall come out of hell-fire.*
>
> *O son of Adam, as long as you call on me and ask, I shall forgive you for what you have done.*
>
> From the sayings of Muhammad

Talk of the devil should perhaps be approached in the same way. On the one hand, although it appears late in the Bible, it occurs very frequently in the teaching of Jesus, in the writings of his first disciples, and in the teaching of Muhammad. Some would happily dismiss it as part of a dated world-view which no longer makes sense to people today.

On the other hand, its frequency in the New Testament and the Qur'an (where he is named Shaytan or Iblis) suggests that the word stands for something real. It does not have to be taken literally, but it does need to be taken seriously. Believers claim that there is a power of evil in the world, far outweighing the sum total of human evil, on which it would be disastrous to turn a blind eye. It is present in all people, the good as well as the bad. To personify this 'demonic' element is to draw attention to its power to reduce the world to chaos if left unchallenged, and to point to a new humanity, where collective goodness begins to predominate over satanic evil.

Conclusion

This chapter began with a warning that talk about the afterlife, by definition, has to be hesitant and approximative. What can be said about life after death is not something we can directly know, but only indirectly infer, deduce and guess.

If our overview of this obscure scenario (survival, immortality, reincarnation, resurrection, heaven, hell, devil) has produced rather more questions than answers, we should not be disappointed, less still surprised. For in this area of theology more than in any other, the disbeliever remains as much in the dark as the believer. Both can only make an act of faith in what they believe, and ask, with the Spanish philosopher and poet Unamuno: Who knows?

In the most secret recess of the spirit of man
who believes that death will put an end to
his personal consciousness
and even to his memory for ever,
in that inner recess, even without his
    knowing it perhaps
a shadow hovers, a vague shadow lurks,
a shadow of a shadow of uncertainty,
and while he tells himself: 'There is nothing
    for it
but to live this passing life, for there is no
    other!'
at the same time he hears, in this most
    secret recess,
his own doubt murmur: 'Who knows?...'
He is not sure he hears aright, but he hears.

Likewise, in some recess of the soul,
of the true believer who has faith in the
    future life,
a muffled voice, the voice of uncertainty,
murmurs in his spirit's ear: 'Who knows?...'
Perhaps these voices are no louder than the
    buzzing of mosquitoes
when the wind roars through the trees in the
    woods;
we scarcely make out the humming and yet,
mingled with the roar of the storm, it can be
    heard.
How, without this uncertainty, could we
    ever live?

M. de Unamuno (1864–1936),
The Tragic Sense of Life

SAMPLE EXAM QUESTIONS

1 Explain the philosophical issues which arise from a belief in resurrection. Does the concept of reincarnation make more sense than the concept of resurrection?

(OCR AS sample paper)

2 'Disembodied existence can never be explained coherently because it is a contradiction in terms.' Discuss.

(OCR A sample paper)

3 'Innocent suffering is impossible to explain unless there is life after death.' Discuss.

(OCR A sample paper)

4 What are said to be the distinctive features of a 'near-death' experience? Explain and assess the claim that such experiences can be dismissed as 'purely subjective'.

(AQA A sample paper)

5 Describe and explain the main features of a belief in an afterlife. Assess the claim that such belief may be seen as a system of 'rewards and punishments' for controlling behaviour in this life.

(AQA A sample paper)

6 Analyse the differences between the survival of the disembodied soul, and belief in resurrection. Assess which of these two beliefs might provide the stronger philosophical basis for a belief in life after death.

(Edexcel A sample paper)

9 God, alive or dead?

Theism is the name given to any system (*ism*) of belief in God (*theos*). **Atheism** is simply the opposite, any system of *dis*belief in God.

ATHEISTIC CHRISTIANS?

THIS definition of atheism, however, is too negative. There are positive aspects of atheism (especially in its modern form) which are more clearly acknowledged in the other 'isms' with which atheism is often synonymous:

- **humanism** which emphasizes the priority to be given to human beings, whose autonomy and freedom is not to be made subject to any system
- **rationalism** which holds that the power of reasoning, which distinguishes humans from the rest of creation, is the criterion of truth, and not any outside authority
- **secularism** which points to the secular or worldly sphere (as distinct from the religious or otherworldly) as the focus of human concern and endeavour.

Paradoxically, there are strong echoes of the Christian Gospel in these ideals. The preaching of Jesus was itself a human and down-to-earth philosophy of this kind, where people mattered more than the sabbath, where Kingdom-Come was a reality to be worked at here and now and not later on, and where the ordinary (not the extraordinary) was the place in which the reality people call 'God' was to be found. In short, Christianity from its earliest days was an incarnational faith, where God was accessible *in carne*, in the flesh. What could be more radically human or secular? No wonder it was condemned by the Roman Empire as a most impudent emptying of the heavens and a most pernicious atheism!

PROTEST

IT is of course also a paradox that a faith which was originally so worldly, down-to-earth and people-centred, was slowly transformed into an authoritarian and otherworldly spirituality, highly suspicious of the human and contemptuous of the world. It was not until the 14th century Renaissance with its rediscovery of human values that dissenting secularist voices were heard. These grew ever more vociferous in the 16th century Reformation with its clarion call for the eradication of many abuses (institutional, financial, sexual, etc.) within Christianity. The 18th century Enlightenment, with its enthusiastic promotion of all the new sciences, brought this protest movement to a climax as one after another of its advocates repudiated the God of traditional religion. Such a God is not only irrelevant (the sciences can explain all that we shall ever need to know) but positively harmful, preventing people from facing reality.

The German philosopher Ludwig Feuerbach (1804–72) was the main protagonist of this point of view. For him, the God of traditional theology was simply a projection of human desires: this is what people themselves would like to be. But by projecting their desires onto the heavens people have diminished themselves and obscured their own divinity. In short, God did not create the human race – the human race created God.

Feuerbach's views were largely responsible for the rejection of religion by Karl Marx (1818–83) – God is a mere instrument of social control and an obstacle to the liberation of the oppressed (see page 72); by Friedrich Nietzsche (1844–1900) – traditional belief in God has enslaved the human race (see page 64); by Sigmund Freud (1856–1939) – God is no more than an infantile security blanket (see page 73); and by Jean-Paul Sartre (1905–80) who said 'If human beings are to live, God must die. If God exists, man is nothing' (*The Devil and the Good God*).

I deny God: for me that means I deny the negation of man... The question concerning the existence or non-existence of God is not important, but the question concerning the existence or non-existence of man is.

Ludwig Feuerbach,
The Essence of Christianity

What sets me apart is not that I recognize no God, either in history or in nature or behind nature – but that I find that which has been revered as God not 'godlike' but pitiable, absurd, harmful, not merely an error but a crime against life. I deny God as God. If this God of the Christians were proved to me to exist, I should know even less how to believe in him.

Friedrich Nietzsche, *The Anti-Christ*

Religious belief is outmoded and ridiculous, a worn-out but once useful crutch in mankind's journey towards truth. We consider the time has come for that crutch to be abandoned.

Professor Peter Atkins, newspaper article

For discussion

Are you totally, partly, or not at all in sympathy with the atheistic views in the box above? Why?

Friedrich Nietzsche 'I deny God as God'

WHAT SORT OF GOD?

IT should be pointed out that, in many cases, the views just referred to do not reject God and religion outright. What they reject is the classical and traditional God, the kind of God and religion that are read about or heard of. This makes it important to repeat the observation made on page 23, that the existence of God is really a secondary question. The question that needs to be dealt with first is the nature of God. You can't answer the question, Does God exist? until you have answered the question, What sort of God are we talking about?

Because of this, a distinction must be made between classical and modern atheism. In the past, atheists have said that the word 'God' does not refer to any reality and never has done. God, however he is defined, is a total illusion, a non-entity.

Many atheists today say something quite different. The God who does not exist, they say, is the God of traditional Christian theology.

Strictly speaking, this kind of atheism should be called anti-theism, an urgent plea for new definitions of God. For there are many definitions of God which *ought* to be repudiated as unsuited for worship (worthship). For example, the God who is so beyond our reach that human reason has no value. Or the God who is so paternalistic that he keeps people infantile. Or the God who is so otherworldly that this world becomes worthless. Or the God who occasionally intervenes in human affairs but is normally absent. Or the God who fills the gaps in our knowledge and whom the progress of science therefore gradually edges out. Or the God whom one acknowledges out of a shrewd sense of insurance. Or the God whom his friends are able to cajole and manipulate. Or the God who is presented as a rival for human affection, as if one has to choose either him or people.

The Roman Catholic Vatican II Council, in its document *The Church in the Modern World* (1965), admitted that much modern atheism has been brought about by Christians themselves, preaching an ungodly God.

> *Believers themselves frequently bear some responsibility for this situation (atheism)... Atheism stems from a variety of causes, including a critical reaction against religious beliefs... Hence believers can have more than a little to do with the birth of atheism... if they conceal rather than reveal the authentic face of God and religion.*
>
> *Documents of Vatican II*

Throughout history, the word 'atheist' has been used as a political smear-word to besmirch those who have challenged the current orthodoxy. Even Jesus and his first followers were called atheists.

Nothing can mask the face of God so effectively as religion.

Martin Buber

The Church can be the Anti-Christ; and when it denies that possibility, it is the Anti-Christ.

Reinhold Niehbur

The musician Artur Rubinstein, interviewed by the BBC shortly before he died (1982), was asked, 'Do you believe in God?'. He replied, 'No, I believe in something much bigger than God. I don't need the sort of God you hear of in sermons. What I need, and which can alone command my respect, awe, gratitude and love, is the power in each of us, and deep in the whole of creation, which is responsible for that miracle that all life is.'

One has to pass through atheism to faith; the old God must be pulverised and forgotten before the new can reveal himself to us.

G. Tyrrell in M. Petre,
Autobiography and Life of George Tyrrell I,
270, Edward Arnold 1912)

THE DEATH OF GOD

THIS chapter can perhaps best be summed up by analysing the phrase 'the death of God', of which there has been much talk since the 1960s. The phrase means rather different things to different people.

For some it means not only that God is dead, but that he has always been dead. What is new is the realization that this is the case. By and large more and more people, especially in the West, have come to the conclusion that there has never been a God and that they and they alone must take responsibility for the running of the world.

For others, the death of God is a peculiarly Christian statement. The God who did exist, once upon a time, eventually emptied himself totally into the life of Jesus of Nazareth. It is this entirely secular and human reality which has replaced the divine, spiritual, timeless, impassive and transcendent God of the Old Testament. Christianity is an explicitly secular and this-worldly faith.

The 'religionless Christianity' of the German theologian Dietrich Bonhoeffer (1906–45) is a variant of this view. He wrote:

God as a working hypothesis in morals, politics or science, has been abolished, and the same thing has happened in philosophy and religion... We cannot be honest unless we recognize that we have to live in the world etsi deus non daretur *(even if, or as if, there were no God). And this is just what we do recognize – before God!... God would have us know that we must live as men who manage to live our lives without him. The God who is with us is the God who forsakes us (as he forsook Jesus on the cross)... Before God and with God we live without God... The Bible directs us to God's powerlessness and suffering; only this kind of God can help... I'm still discovering, right up to this moment, that it is only by living completely in this world that one learns to have faith.*

Letters and Papers from Prison, July 1944

For others still, what has died is not God, either totally or partially, but the idea of God. God has 'gone dead' on them. He is no longer experienced as living, or meaningful, or relevant, but only as silent or even absent. It is the death of this God that many modern atheists proclaim. Many modern theologians welcome this proclamation, and hope that this 'death' may allow the face of the true God to appear.

We owe a debt to Nietzsche, and may one day turn the tables on him in a way he would have appreciated, by saluting him as a great reformer of Christianity.

D. Cupitt, *The Sea of Faith*,
BBC 1984

Perhaps the only real atheist is not the person who rejects the word 'God' (who remains a mystery that no word can ever express), but the person who rejects all reality as absurd and meaningless, and so concludes that words like 'love', 'justice', 'truth', etc., are mere words, standing for nothing. There are very few who would adopt a nihilism as absolute as this.

For discussion

If there was nobody, anywhere, who still believed in God, is there any way in which it would make sense to say God still existed?

Why do you believe (not believe) in God?

- Because I was taught to believe (taught not to believe) in God.
- Because I respect the many eminent people who have believed (who have not believed) in God.
- Because the classical proofs for his existence convince me (do not convince me).
- Because the world we live in cannot be explained (can be explained) without a creator God.
- Because some areas of life (for example miracles) require (do not require) a God.
- Because I find praying to God makes a difference (makes no difference) to me and to the world.
- Because I cannot imagine (I can well imagine) not surviving after death.
- Because the evidence for the World To Come is (is not) overwhelming.
- Because I am convinced (not convinced) by the experience of God others have had.
- Because I have personally experienced (never experienced) God.

Which of these are your own reasons for believing or not believing in God? Can you add other reasons?

SAMPLE EXAM QUESTIONS

1 For what reason might a person today refer to himself/herself as an atheist? To what extent are these reasons similar to, or different from, arguments used by atheists in the past?   (UCLES 1990)

2 After the experience of the 20th century, is agnosticism the most honest response to the question of the existence of God?

(UCLES 1992)

3 'God is dead! Heaven is empty – Weep, children, you no longer have a father' (G. de Nerval). Discuss.

(UCLES 1992)

4 What counter-arguments can be used by an atheist against the 'proofs of God's existence'? How successful are these arguments?

(UCLES 1996)

5 Is the existence of evil a conclusive disproof of the existence of God?

(UCLES 1996)

6 'I do not say there is not a God. I merely say that I have not had that experience' (Albert Camus). Discuss.

(UCLES 1997)

Conclusion

As I said in my foreword, it has been my aim to present the material in this book as impartially as possible. I have tried to represent all views fairly, without taking sides, in order to allow readers to make up their own minds. It is not that I have no views of my own, or even that I wish to keep these views hidden. But I have no desire, or right, to impose these on others, even those with whom I most strongly disagree. Because their point of view has a right to be heard too, and to be presented sympathetically.

I have tried to make it quite clear that I have considerable sympathy with much of the modern protest against religion. The behaviour of believers through history has rarely been such as to arouse the admiration of outsiders. Less still the often unattractive images of the God they claim to serve. Far from deserving odium for rejecting such behaviour and such images, sceptics should be complimented on their good sense. Two Anglican bishops and a Roman Catholic theologian admit as much in the excerpts quoted in the box below – the first from a chapter boldly entitled 'Can a Truly Contemporary Person *Not* be an Atheist?'. It goes without saying that all three authors continue beyond these excerpts to explain why they are still believers.

is one that takes over after the death of God, as 'God' has traditionally been understood.

J. A. T. Robinson, *The New Reformation*

Consider briefly the pile of evidence which suggests that believing in God is bad for humanity... The Crusades, the Inquisition, anti-Semitism... great intra-Christian rivalry... believers displaying loyalty to the Faith by persecution... Looked at coolly, it is plain that, on the basis of their record so far, religious people and institutions are strong persistent contributors to the case for atheism.

D. Jenkins, *Free to Believe*

Man today wants above all to be human. Not a superman, but equally not a sub-man. He wants to be completely human in a world as human as possible... Man has taken under his control much – indeed, almost everything – for which God, superhuman and supramundane powers and spirits were supposed to be responsible, and has truly come of age... It is possible to deny God. Atheism cannot be eliminated rationally. It is unproved, but it is also irrefutable... There are no positive arguments for the impossibility of atheism. If someone says there is no God, his claim cannot be positively refuted.

H. Küng, *On Being A Christian*

There is an important sense in which a person who is fully a man of our times must – or, at any rate, may – be an atheist before he can be a Christian. That is to say, there is so much in the atheist's case which is true that, for many people today, the only Christian faith which can be valid for them

That much needs to be said on behalf of the true God (if he exists) who lies hidden behind the clumsy language and ungodly behaviour of believers. Scepticism and atheism have played an important role in purifying theism, for which believers should be grateful.

On the other hand, if believers ought to show more respect for sceptics, the converse is also true. Sceptics have no right to be dismissive of believers, as if their convictions were of little value, being 'only' beliefs. It is true God cannot be proved. But it is also true that he cannot be disproved. Atheism cannot escape the stigma of also being called 'only a belief' – because atheism is not a *refusal* to believe that God exists, it is itself a *belief* that God does not exist. The difference is important.

If faith can be belittled by saying it is no more than a projection, why should one not say the same of atheism? Is it not possible that wanting God *not* to exist could be as much a fantasy as hoping that God *does* exist?

Neither faith nor reason, neither religion nor science, neither belief nor disbelief, has a monopoly of the truth. Neither has the right to ridicule, belittle or domineer the other. Each has a right to be respected. Each has insights to which the other must listen. Both need to enter ever more deeply into dialogue, and to learn from each other. There does not need to be a gulf between the two, even though different people will want to draw the dividing line differently. After all, the marvellously complex reality which each of the two is trying to understand is exactly the same. Why should either imagine that there is only one valid interpretation of that one reality?

For discussion

You are a believer. If, for whatever reason, you came to the conclusion that God does not exist, what would change in your life?

You are a non-believer. If, for whatever reason, you came to the conclusion that God exists, what would change in your life?

Further reading

Armstrong, K., *A History of God*, Mandarin, 1993

Clarke, P., *Questions about God*, Stanley Thorne, 1999

Cole, P., *Philosophy of Religion*, Abacus, 1994

Cole, P., and Lee, J., *Religious Language*, Abacus, 1995

Cupitt, D., *Taking Leave of God*, SCM, 1980

Davies, B., *Introduction to Philosophy of Religion*, OUP, 1993

Dawkins, R., *The Blind Watchmaker*, Longman, 1986

The Selfish Gene, OUP, 1989

Donovan, R., *Religious Language*, Prentice, 1983

Encyclopedia of World Religions, Phoebus, 1975

Evans, C., *Philosophy of Religion*, IVP, 1985

Gaarder, J., *Sophie's World*, Phoenix House, 1995

Hick, J. (ed.), *The Existence of God*, Macmillan, 1964

Evil and the God of Love, Macmillan, 1964

(ed.), *Truth and Dialogue*, Sheldon, 1975

Death and Eternal Life, Macmillan, 1985

Philosophy of Religion, Prentice Hall, 1990

Honderich, T. (ed.), *Oxford Companion to Philosophy*, OUP, 1995

Hull, J., *Sense and Nonsense about God*, SCM, 1974

James, W., *The Varieties of Religious Experience*, Penguin, 1983

Jones, S., *Almost Like a Whale*, Doubleday, 1999

Jordan, A., Lockyer, N. and Tate, E., *Philosophy of Religion*, Stanley Thorne, 1999

Küng, H., *Eternal Life?*, SCM, 1991

Does God Exist?, SCM, 1995

Lewis, H., *Philosophy of Religion*, English University Press, 1965

MacQuarrie, J., *Twentieth Century Religious Thought*, SCM, 1963

God Talk, SCM, 1967

Mitchell, B., *Philosophy of Religion*, OUP, 1971

Moltmann, J., *God in Creation*, SCM, 1985

Mullen, R., *Thinking about Religion*, Hodder, 1991

Osborne, R., *Philosophy for Beginners*, Writers and Readers, 1992

Pailin, D., *Groundwork of Philosophy of Religion*, Epworth, 1986

Peacocke, A., *Theology for a Scientific Age*, SCM, 1993

Peters, T. (ed.), *Science and Theology*, Perseus Books, 1998

Pittenger, N., *God in Process*, SCM, 1967

Polkinghorne, J., *The Faith of a Physicist*, Princeton University, 1994

Poole, M., *A Guide to Science and Belief*, Lion, 1994

Raeper, W. and Smith, L., *Beginner's Guide to Ideas*, Lion, 1991

Ramsey, I., *Religious Language*, SCM, 1957

Richards, H., *What Happens When You Pray?*, SCM, 1980

The Miracles of Jesus, 23rd Publications, 1986

The First Easter, 23rd Publications, 1986

Death and After, 23rd Publications, 1987

Richardson, A. (ed.), *New Dictionary of Christian Theology*, SCM, 1983

Robinson, J., *Honest to God*, SCM, 1963

Exploration into God, SCM, 1967

Scruton, R., *An Intelligent Person's Guide to Philosophy*, Duckworth, 1996

Smart, J. and Haldane, J., *Atheism and Theism*, Blackwell, 1996

Smart, N., *Philosophers and Religious Truth*, SCM, 1964

(ed.), *Nineteenth Century Religious Thought in the West*, OUP, 1998

Swinburne, R., *The Existence of God*, OUP, 1979

Faith and Reason, OUP, 1981

Revelation, OUP, 1992

Thompson, M., *Religion and Science (Advanced Teaching Pack)*, Hodder, 1995

Tilghman, B., *Introduction to Philosophy of Religion*, Blackwell, 1994

Tyler, S., *A-Level Religious Studies: Philosophy of Religion and Christian Belief*, Ball, 1996

Vardy, P., *The Puzzle of Evil*, Fount, 1992

The Puzzle of God, Fount, 1995

Ward, K., *God, Chance and Necessity*, One World, 1996

Webber, J., *Faith and Reason*, Abacus, 1995

Revelation and Religious Experience, Abacus, 1995

Wiles, M., *What is Theology?*, OUP, 1976

Wilson, A., *God's Funeral*, John Murray, 1999

Glossary

Note – Words appearing in **bold** within an entry have their own entry elsewhere in the glossary.

Agape   The word used in the New Testament for the kind of love that God has for humans – outgoing and seeking only their welfare.

Agnosticism   'Not knowing'. Agnostics claim it is not possible to *know* whether what religion refers to is real or not.

Analogy   The Greek word *analogia* means similarity. Words are called analogical when their meaning is similar (though not exactly the same) when used in different circumstances. All human language about God is analogical.

Analytic   In **linguistic philosophy**, statements are called analytic if they can be shown to be true or false by simply *analysing* the meaning of the words (e.g. 'Two plus two equals four').

Anthropic Principle   The principle which states that the cosmos can be shown to be purposely orientated towards producing human beings (*anthropoi*).

Anthropogenesis   The word used by Teilhard de Chardin to speak of the *genesis* or appearance of human beings (*anthropoi*) as the climax of the **evolution**ary process.

Anthropomorphism   The use of human (*anthropoi*) terms (*morphe*) to speak of God.

Anti-theism   Any system which is opposed to (*anti*) **theism**.

Apophatic   The Greek word given to the theology which strongly insists that God is not (*apo*) captured by what we say (*phatis*) about him.

A posteriori   An argument which is based on (or after, *post*) something which has actually been experienced.

A priori   An argument which is based on a general principle, before (*prior*) any experience or evidence is produced.

Atheism   A system of belief that denies the existence of God (*theos*).

Autonomy   Rule or dominion (*nomos*) coming from within a person or community (*autos*), not from outside.

Biogenesis   The term used by Teilhard de Chardin for the first appearance (*genesis*) of life (*bios*) in the process of **evolution**.

Cartesian   The adjectival form of the name Descartes.

Categorical Imperative   A term used by Kant to express the over-riding (categorical) sense of obligation (**imperium**) which makes us act only on what we would wish to be a universal law.

Chaos Theory   The recent scientific pro-position that the universe, even though it continues to form an orderly whole, is not made up of building blocks obeying strict laws, but of random waves and impulses.

Christogenesis   Teilhard de Chardin's word for the emergence or *genesis* of Christ as the high point of humanity, thus revealing the meaning of the whole process of **evolution**.

Christology   The study (*logos*) of the significance of Jesus Christ for Christian faith.

Clairvoyance   The ability clearly to perceive (*voir*) things beyond the range of the senses.

Concordism   The theory that recent scientific discoveries, far from disagreeing with the Bible, are totally in *concord*ance with the text.

Contingent   The Latin word *contingere* means to happen. Things are said to be contingent when they happen to take place, but need not. The word is the opposite of necessary.

Continuous Creation The theory, common until the 1960s that the continuing expansion of the universe (in spite of the 'steady state' of its density) requires the continuing creation of new matter. The theory has today given way to Hubble's theory of a single 'creation event'.

Conversion In religious terms, the turning (*versio*) from disbelief to belief.

Cosmological Associated with the *cosmos* or universe. The arguments for the existence of God that are based on facts about the cosmos we live in, are called cosmological.

Creationism The belief that all species of living beings were from the beginning created distinct from each other, rather than evolving from each other. Also called **Fixism**.

Deduction A conclusion which logically and necessarily follows from (*ductum de*) the preceding premises. It is a stronger form of argument than **induction**, where the conclusion is only *in*ferred from a number of instances.

Deism The belief in the rather cold and impersonal God (*deus*) deducible by reason alone, as distinct from being revealed. It is often contrasted with the warmer word **theism**.

Demythologization An unhappy word, which suggests that **myth** must be eliminated in order to discover the real meaning of a story. More correctly, it refers to the acceptance of myth as myth, and not as a piece of history. This allows the myth to speak in the way that stories can speak, even when they are not meant to be taken literally.

Determinism The belief that all events are totally predetermined by other events and that freedom of choice is an illusion.

Dialectic The Greek word means dialogue, and is used in philosophy to describe a process in which two opposites are brought into confrontation in order to fuse the best of both into something higher.

Dualism The belief that the world is ruled by two (*duo*) eternally conflicting powers, one good and one evil.

Ego The Latin word for 'I' is used in psychology to refer to the conscious self as keeping a balance between the **superego** and the **id**.

Empirical comes from a Greek word referring to experience. It is used in philosophy to refer to what is known by experience rather than theory, and so can be tested and verified. An empiricist is one who denies the reality of anything that cannot be tested.

Equivocal Words which sound *equal* or the same, but have a totally different meaning, are called equivocal. The phrase 'beat it' does not mean to a cook what it means to an intruder.

Eros The Greek word for the love which seeks the beloved only for its own benefit, unlike **agape**.

Evolution means unfolding, and is used to describe the slow process by which minute changes in a few living beings, continuing for thousands of years, have produced countless species quite distinct from each other.

Extrasensory Perception (ESP) The receiving of information by means other than (*extra*) the use of the senses.

Faith Faith, or belief, is usually contrasted with reason and evidence. Some truths we hold because we are led to them by reason and evidence. Others we accept on the authority of those in whom we have confidence. One is not more certain than the other. Most people live with both kinds of truth.

Fixism See **Creationism**.

Freewill Solution One of the many 'solutions' to the problem of evil. God cannot be blamed for the world's evil, which is entirely due to human freedom to choose between good and evil.

Fundamentalism The name chosen by conservative Protestants at the beginning of the 20th century to defend the *fundamentals* of Christianity against the new **Liberalism**. In interpreting the Bible they emphasize its **inerrancy**, and tend to take it as rigidly and literally as possible.

Henotheism The belief in many gods, of whom only one (*henos*) is chosen to be worshipped.

Hesed A Hebrew word used to express the mercy and compassion which define God.

Humanism A philosophy which regards humans (not God or the Church) as the centre of reference, interest and concern.

Id The Latin word for 'it' is used in psychology to refer to the unconscious primitive and instinctual urges which the **ego** tries to control.

Immanent A word used of God to express the belief that he remains (*manens*) within the universe, and is not distant from it.

Immaterial, incorporeal One of the classical attributes of God, as not being formed of *matter* or having a body (*corpus*) in the manner of physical objects.

Immeasurable, immense One of the classical attributes of God, as being unable to be measured.

Immortality Literally 'non-death'. This quality belongs to God by definition. It is attributed by some philosophers also to angels and human souls, as being of such a nature that they will exist for ever.

Immutable One of the classical attributes of God, as unable to change or *mutate* for the better (or the worse).

Impassible One of the classical attributes of God as not susceptible to suffering (*passio*).

Incarnation A Christian word, used to express the belief that God's relationship with the world is *in* the very flesh (*caro*) of human history, and that this was best exemplified in the life of Jesus of Nazareth.

Incomprehensible One of the classical attributes of God, as unable to be *comprehended* or grasped by the mind.

Incorporeal See **Immaterial**.

Induction See **Deduction**.

Ineffable A word used to speak of God as the mystery which cannot be expressed (*effari*).

Inerrancy A quality sometimes attributed to the Bible as being free of *error*, at least on matters which its authors thought important.

Infinite One of the classical attributes of God, as having no limits (*fines*).

Invisible One of the classical attributes of God, as being a reality which cannot be physically seen (*visio*).

Kalam A 10th century school of Muslim theology which maintained, against strong opposition, that the existence of God can be known (even without divine revelation) by the God-given power of human reason or argument (*kalam*).

Language games The name given by Wittgenstein to his claim that the uses of language are governed by rules, as games are. To find the meaning you must know which game is being played.

Liberalism The name given to the interpretation of the Bible which is more free or *liberal* than that of the **fundamentalists**. Liberal scholars insist that all relevant literary and historical questions must be asked before we can know the meaning of the text.

Linguistic philosophy The branch of philosophy which deals with the meaning of statements. See **Logical Positivism**.

Literalism The understanding of words and statements in their literal sense. Clearly many texts of the Bible are meant to be taken literally, but few Christians would nowadays question the fact that some texts were meant from the beginning to be taken as fiction, story or poetry.

Logical Positivism The belief (unverifiable) that the only true statements are those that can be verified, and that those that cannot (like many religious statements) are neither true nor false, but simply meaningless.

Metempsychosis See **Reincarnation**.

Miracle is often defined as an event which violates the laws of nature and so points to a supernatural origin. But the biblical use of the word is not so rigid and refers to any wonderful event (*mirum*) which makes believers praise the God of surprises.

Monism The belief in one (*monos*) eternal Principle, not two (see **Dualism**).

Monolatry The worship (*latria*) of only one God (*monos*) among the many that are thought to exist.

Monotheism The belief in a single (*monos*) God, excluding any other claim to the title.

Myth In the philosophy of religion, the word 'myth' does not have the negative overtones it has elsewhere. Myths are superhuman stories which people have always told to express how they understand their world and their place in it. Such stories are heavy with meaning, which can be lost if they are taken literally.

Natural Selection Darwin's term for the process by which **evolution** apparently takes place. Nature herself as it were 'selects' those living beings that survive, with the result that only the fittest produce the next generation.

Near-Death Experiences See **Out-of-Body Experiences**.

Noogenesis Teilhard de Chardin's word for the *genesis* or emergence of self-awareness (*nous*) in the process of the **evolution** of matter.

Objective Existing in the real world of *objects*, independently of the observer.

Obscurantism Any system which opposes new knowledge, and prefers to keep the real state of affairs *obscure*.

Omega Point The name given by Teilhard de Chardin to the final (*omega*) stage of the **evolution**ary process, when struggle will cease and final harmony is achieved.

Omnipotent One of the classical attributes of God, who is said to be able (*potens*) to do everything (*omne*).

Omnipresent One of the classical attributes of God, as being present everywhere and absent nowhere.

Omniscient One of the classical attributes of God, who is said to be knowing (*sciens*) of all (*omne*) – in the present, past and future.

Ontological Relating to the nature of being (*ontos*), whether of creatures or of God.

Out-of-Body Experiences (OBE) Experiences which some people claim to have undergone in 'another world' while their bodies remained in this world.

Panentheism In contrast with **pantheism** (which makes no distinction between God and the universe) and with **theism** (which tends to look for God outside the universe), panentheism states that everything (*pan*) is in (*en*) God (*theos*), and God is in everything.

Pantheism The belief that there is no distinction between God and the universe, and that God is everything that exists (*pan*).

Paranormal A word used of experiences that are outside (*para*) the normal and which are often ascribed to the influence of another world.

Philosophy means the love (*phil*) of wisdom (*sophia*) and includes any critical investigation into what is true and real.

Polytheism The belief in many (*poly*) gods, each responsible for a different department of life.

Positivism The nineteenth century philosophy that claimed that the only true knowledge is knowledge that can be tested. The rest is mere speculation.

Probability and Proof The English word 'probable' is ambiguous. Although etymologically it means the same as 'proof' (viz. prove-able) the word is weaker in actual usage, and even a high degree of probability (99.9 recurring %), impressive as it is, and more than adequate as a working hypothesis, cannot be regarded as equal to a solid proof.

Process Theology The theology that assumes that, since all reality is a dynamic *process* rather than an unchanging static state, so the ultimate Reality of God must be a process of becoming. He not only affects everything that happens, but is himself affected by it. See **Panentheism**.

Psyche The Greek word for soul is used in psychology to refer to the unconscious self, which can become conscious by the use of psychoanalysis.

Psychokinesis (PK) The ability claimed by some to be able to move (*kinesis*) objects by the power of the mind alone (*psyche*).

Rahamim A remarkable word frequently used of God's love in the Hebrew Bible. It refers to the tenderness that a mother feels for a child in her womb.

Rationalism The belief that human reason (*ratio*) is the criterion of truth, not any outside authority.

Reincarnation (Latin) or **Metempsychosis** (Greek). The re-embodiment (*caro*) of the soul (*psyche*) in another form after death.

Resurrection means 'rising again', and refers in theology to the bodily returning to life of the dead. This is claimed by Christians to be true not only of the Jesus who died on a cross, but eventually of all who are incorporated into the risen Christ.

Revelation The removal of a veil (*velum*) from something which has been hidden. In religion it refers to God's disclosure of himself and his purpose for the human race.

Righteousness A word much used in the Bible to refer to God's uprightness and justness. In English the word has a cold legal ring, as if God was just to some law. But in Hebrew it simply means that God is just to himself, and therefore consistently gracious and merciful.

Secularism The belief that the secular or worldly sphere, as distinct from the religious or otherworldly, should be the focus of human interest and endeavour.

Steady State See **Continuous Creation**.

Subjective Existing only in the observer or *subject*, not in outside reality.

Superego In psychology, the *superi*or part of the mind which acts, usually under parental and religious influence, as a person's conscience.

Supernova One of the fruits of the scientific investigation into the origins of the universe has been the discovery of supposedly 'new' (*nova*) stars, which have continued to erupt and flare in space throughout time. The *super*nova are particularly large examples which not only erupt but self-destruct and form galaxies of their own. The sun and its satellite earth are the end product of one of these explosions millions of years ago.

Synthetic In linguistic philosophy, statements are called synthetic if they can be put alongside (*syn-thesis*) observation and testing to find out whether they are true or false.

Teleological Arguing from the end or purpose (*telos*) of something to its origin.

Theism The word comes from the Greek *theos*, and should mean simply a system which believes in God. Inevitably over the years it has come to refer to the rather abstract God of philosophy.

Theodicy The justification (*diké*) of God (*theos*) against objections raised by the existence of evil.

Theology The study (*logos*) of the existence, nature and purpose of God (*theos*).

Theosphere Another name for Teilhard de Chardin's **Omega Point**, when God (*theos*) will be all in all.

Transcendent A word used to express the mystery of God, who is beyond (*trans*) all description or definition.

Transformism An earlier word for **evolution**, emphasizing the observation that organisms are gradually *transformed* by the environment in which they grow up.

Univocal Words are called univocal when they always have one (*uni*) and the same meaning, wherever they are used. A spade is a spade is a spade.

Verification The testing of a statement to find out whether it is true (*verum*).

Via negativa An acknowledgement that our meagre positive knowledge of God may be supplemented by a number of *negatives*: he is not *x*, not *y*, etc.

Index